A STORY LARGER
THAN MY OWN

✳

A STORY LARGER
THAN MY OWN

WOMEN WRITERS LOOK BACK ON
THEIR LIVES AND CAREERS

Edited by Janet Burroway

THE UNIVERSITY OF CHICAGO PRESS
CHICAGO AND LONDON

JANET BURROWAY is the author of eight novels, including *The Buzzards* and *Raw Silk*; two best-selling textbooks, *Writing Fiction* and *Imaginative Writing*; and the memoir *Losing Tim*. She is also the author of numerous plays, short stories, poetry collections, and children's books. She is Robert O. Lawton Distinguished Professor Emerita at Florida State University and divides her time between Lake Geneva, Wisconsin, and Chicago.

The University of Chicago Press, Chicago 60637
The University of Chicago Press, Ltd., London
© 2014 by Janet Burroway
All rights reserved. Published 2014.
Printed in the United States of America

23 22 21 20 19 18 17 16 15 14   1 2 3 4 5

ISBN-13: 978-0-226-01407-4 (cloth)
ISBN-13: 978-0-226-01410-4 (paper)
ISBN-13: 978-0-226-01424-1 (e-book)
DOI: 10.7208/chicago/9780226014241.001.0001

Library of Congress Cataloging-in-Publication Data

A story larger than my own : women writers look back on their lives and careers / edited by Janet Burroway.
    pages ; cm
    ISBN 978-0-226-01407-4 (cloth : alkaline paper) — ISBN 978-0-226-01410-4 (paperback : alkaline paper) — ISBN 978-0-226-01424-1 (e-book) 1. Women authors, American—Literary collections. I. Burroway, Janet.
    PS151.S76 2014
    810.9'9287—dc23

                        2013032197

♾ This paper meets the requirements of ANSI/NISO Z39.48-1992 (Permanence of Paper).

CONTENTS

INTRODUCTION

I entered the millennium at age sixty-four, conscious that I was lucky. I had on the third try secured a happy marriage. I had published a dozen books and had not lost my lust for writing. My two boys, both born abroad and always travelers, had settled in London and Namibia with their families, so that Peter and I joked we were "forced to travel." I knew the carnival had an uncertain end date, but I felt the force of words I have used already: secure, settled, lucky; marriage, books, boys.

But in my late sixties I went through a series of disrupting and disorienting events. I retired after thirty years of teaching literature and creative writing at Florida State. My eldest, Tim, went as a mine-removal trainer to Iraq, returned disillusioned to Namibia, and, like far too many who endured that war, took his own life in the spring of 2004. Three years later, feeling an amorphous but powerful need for change, Peter and I bought a house in the woods in Wisconsin, where I believed I would count out my days in solitary work, starting with a memoir of Tim.

But when we discovered that Chicago was reachable by a short Metra line, I began to find myself solaced by, and ambitious for, the theater, which was thriving in that city and which had been my first love as a writer. I joined Chicago Dramatists, and then Midwest New Musicals. I wrote the memoir, but I also revived a rash-seeming, decades-old desire to write a musical. I acquired the rights to adapt Barry Unsworth's novel *Morality Play* and took on the book and lyrics in partnership with a composer literally fifty years my junior.

A colleague at Florida State, contemplating her own retirement, once told me, "I can't *wait* to be an amateur again," and this now became my mantra. I found enriching pleasure in collaboration, experiment, improvisation. I relished peer pressure and peer praise. I wanted the brevity and driven dialogue of drama. I wanted the brief boxed requisites of the musical lyric.

But these pleasures came at a perplexing cost. I was reasonably well known as a novelist, better known as an author of textbooks, but a virtual novice as a playwright/lyricist. I *liked* being on the student side of the podium after so many years as a teacher. But there's no denying it bruised my ego, or that there arose an exhausting notion of "breaking into" theater like the twenty-four-year-old I'd been at the Yale School of Drama in 1960.

For all these reasons I hungered to hear from older women writers about the trajectory of their writing lives. I sought out several friends, and then women I did not know but aspired to know, and proposed that we should speak to our late-life concerns as a panel at the Association of Writers and Writing Programs (AWP) meeting in 2008. We have so much to say to beginners, I argued, about how to begin. But we rarely ask for the view from the far reaches of a career. Are there insights that could prove useful to a writer further along, at a different fork, with a later start, a new ambition or in different doldrums? What lasts, what changes, what matters, what is the story of a writing life?

This collection of essays grew out of that initial panel discussion and two more that followed at AWP in 2009 and 2012, all of them entitled "Women Writers of a Certain Age." Several of the pieces in this book come, in expanded or different form, from the remarks of women who took part in those discussions. Others I asked to contribute because I admired their work and wanted their perspectives. Most of the essays were written expressly for *A Story Larger than My Own*, though some have been published in other venues. Margaret Atwood's keynote address at the 2012 AWP conference—with its memories of learning craft in the days before creative writing programs or computers—seemed directly on point. Other pieces vary widely in genre and focus; a few are essays in poetry, some are meditations on a single theme, some offer a compressed autobiographical sweep. Some concentrate on the early sources of ambition, some on the discontents or discoveries of middle age, some on the trials and consolations of late life. We have tried to ensure that the book reflects the diversity of women writers of this generation, and are confident that those in following decades will be more diverse still.

All of us here represented were born in the thirties, forties, and early fifties, and both our gender and the timing matter to the larger story. We came of age in the decades that morphed from crinoline petticoat to vintage voile to bell bottoms. The eldest of us were likely to go through four years of university in the somewhat uneasy belief that education would make us better mothers and that we could always "write on the side." The younger wrote manifestos and held vigils against the bomb, their college years drenched in protest songs and the threat of Vietnam. All of us experienced the rise of women's liberation, from *The Feminine Mystique* to *Ms.* to *The Madwoman in the Attic*.

These were years of embryonic change for women who wanted to write and to be taken seriously in the world of letters, who waited for the mail in the fret of an expectant lover, or pushed, tenuous and frustrated, and then insistent and aggrieved, not against any such lofty thing as a glass ceiling but against the scuffed doors of newsrooms, editors, and agents. It worked. We made our way into publishing with an anxious determination that young women of this twenty-first century would find bizarre. But Jane Smiley can write that toward the end of that era she emerged with "not one single thought about whether a girl should be doing this."

In these stories over and over again I encounter my own story being told—what poet Elinor Wilner in another context calls "significant simultaneity." Those of us entering the lit market in the fifties were apt to find, with Maxine Kumin, that women were considered "intellectually inferior, mere appendages in the world of belles letters," or with Hilda Raz that we "seemed not to be welcome in the halls of academe." We might be asked about our virginity like Madeleine Blais, or be told to find a sugar daddy, as one *Herald Tribune* personnel manager in Paris advised me. Just as Gloria Steinham famously posed as a Playboy bunny, so Blais as a young reporter impersonated an airline hostess ("Fly me!"), and I entered a Miss Universe contest to get a news feature on backstage squabbles for the *Phoenix Gazette*.

Feeling alien in a publishing industry inhabited by the literary counterparts of Mad Men, many of us started out writing true romance like Atwood or light verse like Kumin and Hilma Wolitzer. Unlike Kumin, I never had to produce an affidavit from my husband's employer as to the originality of my verses, but I remember signing myself "Jan Burroway" in the hope that I might be mistaken for a man and therefore taken for a *writer*. I also remember finding it tiresome that I kept being "discovered" (until I was well into my thirties) by kindly old gentlemen of the book biz.

One overarching theme of these essays is, unsurprisingly, the world of story and storytelling, and this theme is strikingly interlinked with family, for good and ill, so that Laura Tohe can write both that "my imagination yearned to fly beyond the pages of *Birds of North America*" and that she later realized how "my writing life really began with the stories my relatives told." Furious rebellion against mothers is usual, as is a later realization, regretful or welcome or both, of how much these mothers mattered, and how bravely they endured life stories more fettered than the writers' own. Recalling one such story, Judith Ortiz Cofer quotes Virginia Woolf, "A woman writing thinks back through her mothers," and adds, "and forward through her daughters."

In the meantime, growing up "on the rez" or in small towns and suburbs, many of us like, Patricia Henley, "couldn't wait to get out of there, to places with more shine." Like Marilyn Krysl, we could say of our parents that we "loved them, but their lives seemed tiny and circumscribed." This hunger for a larger personal story could come as an ambition inherent

from childhood, or it could erupt in middle age as a restless-
ness—*is this all?* For Julia Alvarez it came as a fierce identification with Scheherazade: "I needed to internalize this plucky
woman to get where I was going." For my own part, growing
up in the Arizona desert, it came early as an understanding
that I did not belong in that arid landscape and would have to
get *out* and *away* to find my proper place. I longed for trees,
water, cities. It did not occur to me that I would never know
where I do belong, so that like Raz I find myself in a perpetual
state of "not being at home," a familiar sense of exile among
storytellers.

Our confidence grew not only with publication but through
close relationships with nurturing editors, and paradoxically
with the repeated pattern of rejection and recovery, bad reviews ("against which," Wolitzer notes, "there is no defense"),
and survival—always by means of going back to work. Confidence came with public appearance for both Edith Pearlman
("My first gig was in a bar") and Honor Moore ("walking up
the hill in the Berkshires, placing my poems on a stump").

Public appearance was always a bellwether of my own literary sass or timidity as well. For me the significant form of
story came from the films of the forties—the dramatic form
I would return to so much later. My parents loved the movies
and took me to perhaps two double features a week through
my whole childhood. My mother had wanted to be an actress
but was thwarted by her parents on the grounds of health (and
the old conviction that actresses are wicked). Both she and I
wished that I were Shirley Temple. She was, perhaps in rebellion, more than willing to be a stage mother, which was exactly the mother I wanted. She was also an elocution teacher,
and coached me for the Friday night church socials where I

spoke little "pieces" in verse and prose, alternating with the tap-dancing Robinson twins. On these occasions I developed an emotional pattern of dread (*why did I let myself in for this?*), followed by acceptance of the inevitable (*oh, well, here I go*), followed by the pleasures of relief and praise (*it's over, and they liked me!*). This pattern has never entirely left me, in the classroom, readings, speeches—any occasion that required what Toi Derricotte calls "a gracious person smiling." The pattern became a familiar, so that in more confident times I could almost enjoy the stage fright and know I would get through it without collapsing, vomiting, or dying at the podium.

Is it by historical accident that the rise of feminism and the burgeoning of creative writing programs coincided? It is certainly the case that as universities began to embrace the teaching of imaginative writing, they offered a sinecure, and sometimes inspiration, to poets and fiction writers who could not earn a living by writing itself. University reading series, conferences, and groups like the AWP fostered travel, collegiality, and artistic cross-pollination. Contact with young people kept us young. Most of the sniping at writing workshops came from outsiders with scant experience of them.

Still, though many and probably a majority of the women represented in these pages have made their living in such programs, few opted to write here about that lion's share of their thought and time. I hazard that this is because, no matter how much we cared for our students, and we did; no matter how devotedly we taught, read, graded, and counseled (and we were raised as Good Girls who did all those things), teaching was always to a greater or lesser degree in conflict with the time and desire to write. Teaching takes the same parts of the brain that writing does, an alert combination of intuition and analysis, and a brain so employed is drained by the end of the day.

Of course, university teaching offers the crucial opportunity of long summer vacations, and many of us did most of our writing then. I took, when I accepted my first full-time teaching job, a private but deliberate vow that I would not let my lifestyle get out of hand in such a way that I had to teach in the summer. I broke the vow only twice in thirty years, the summer before each of my boys entered college and I was hit with the tuition bill. I was always deeply grateful for these summers, and I was always thrashing against the August deadline. As a novelist I found that even a generous four-month summer was too short to write a novel, and the eight months of courses, counseling, and committee work between those summers was too long to keep the flame of it alive, so that in effect I started over every May. The result was that I might nurture five hundred students in the time it took me to coax one novel into being. And yet I called teaching my *job*, and writing my *work*.

The jobs are fewer now. The four-decade burgeoning of creative writing programs contains a paradox that is perhaps its own destruction. In the new century creative writing is firmly established as a university subject and is often the bread-and-butter major as well as a featured graduate program of diminished English and Humanities departments. But its very popularity has produced a market glut of people trained to teach it who must now seek jobs, either in established programs that can demand extraordinary credentials, or in smaller liberal arts colleges where basic composition is a usual assignment and the course load is all-consuming.

A similar paradox besets the publishing industry. The old establishment of the world of letters was often and insultingly avuncular, but like family it had some other point than profit. Over the period of our adult lives, as women have entered with increasing ease both the creative and the production sides of publishing, we have also seen the trade houses of Boston and New York merge into a corporate monolith that looks for sanction to stockholders rather than to readers and critics. More than one woman in this book mourns the long-term, nurturing relationship between editor and author that used to be a first-book birthright, and is now a thing of the past. Meanwhile, problems of intellectual property and on-line marketing, of appropriation and profitability, bedevil the trade publisher and the writer alike. The tech revolution that has humbled both the music and the newspaper industries has thrown publishing into turmoil. No one knows the future of the printed word. And when "the count" is actually taken, the number of women writers in the culture is still far from proportional. VIDA, an organization founded in 2009 by poets Erin Belieu and Cate Marvin, tracks the gender imbalance in works published and reviewed in major literary magazines. When we view their results, we see that we have come a long way and also not very far.

So where are we, we old women writers, in the world today?

There is in these pages, in nearly every essay, an acknowledgment of the body, its pleasures, but, inevitably, its decline, and of coming to terms with this decline—in the words of Linda Pastan, "the way I always come to terms with things: by writing about them." "The call of the body . . . " Moore ponders. "My fading body," mourns Alicia Ostriker. "How do I know who I am except how it feels to be inside this truck of a body?" asks Derricotte. "Body my house, my horse, my hound," Raz quotes May Swenson, "what will I do when you are fallen"? Rosellen Brown notes "the speed and depth of our losses," which for Kumin includes "about a noun a day." Erica Jong wryly identifies "the final taboo," growing old, while Wolitzer sees the next generation "coming up like chorus girls."

Yet there is at this end of the spectrum a decided sense of freedom in the sense of being "unencumbered by that consuming ambition," as Wolitzer puts it. Gail Godwin has "accepted that my supine dithering is fertile," whereas she perceives herself growing stingier in "the degree of compromise I am willing to inflict on my work in order to see it in print." Even ageism and the corporatization of the publishing industry have their silver linings: among these writers generally there is a willingness to embrace (and sometimes run) the literary magazines, small presses, e-books, and online sites that have inherited much of what used to be called "serious" writing. We go back to work grateful, like Pearlman, for "the ecstasy . . . of writing down words in sequence," knowing with Brown that success *will not satisfy us* and with Henley that "bliss lies in the moment you pluck a metaphor from thin air."

We are in many ways a transitional generation, not only between the fifties and postfeminism, but between carbon paper and cyberspace, ink and ether. We are not altogether (and not equally) optimistic about the human race, or about the capacity of the planet to survive our draconian demands. We are aware that society is still ageist, and that therefore, having won a place at the table, we are somewhat disinvited.

Still, you will find gratitude that we have been able to foster an inner life and find the means to turn it into art. These pages are mostly exploratory. They are anything but prescriptive. The few phrases you will find couched in the imperative mode tend either to the comic ("Just call me Mrs. Pepys"; "Someone, tell me this is a typo") or else to the cosmic and large of heart:

"Call it winter."
"Say yes."
"Undo the folded lie."
"Write what you are afraid to write."
"Keep passing it on."

But the paucity of directive does not mean a lack of guidance. Certain themes recur with the force of life lessons, and it is my hope that the gathering of these long-view images, recollections, and reflections will prove to have a two-fold purpose: the limning of a particular piece of historical experience; and encouragement, identification, and implicit advice for writers of any age and gender.

Janet Burroway

*

JULIA ALVAREZ

1

At difficult times in my writing life, I tell myself certain stories to remind myself of things I mustn't forget, information which can only be encoded in story form or it won't get where it's going. That place I used to call the heart, and which I now call my soul, the heart you earn as you grow old.

As a younger writer, the story I repeated over and over to myself was that of Scheherazade in the sultan's court. Fresh out of her apprenticeship, years spent learning stories in her father's library, now it was time to prove herself by saving her life (to me, earning a livelihood seemed equivalent at the time) and the lives of other women in the kingdom (opening paths for Latina writers gave my own struggles meaning). What larger pressure than having to captivate a sultan who was determined to cut your head off in the morning?

I needed to internalize this plucky woman to get where I was going. But I am relieved that her tenure as my leading muse is over. I could not bear her grueling all-nighters; neither do I have her seductive powers to mesmerize a sultan reader anymore.

Now that I am an older writer, I find myself often in the underworld, burying my dead, getting acquainted with my next stage, my own death. The story I keep returning to for guidance is that of Demeter, Persephone, and Hades.

It is a story of death and rebirth on earth but also in an individual's life. Young Persephone is carried away by Hades, the king of the underworld; her mother, Demeter, goddess of agriculture and the earth's fertility, is bereft. In a fury of self-destructiveness, she punishes her own kingdom with plagues and droughts. Plants, creatures, humans begin to die off. Alarmed, the king of the gods, Zeus, orders that Persephone be returned, provided she hasn't eaten anything in the underworld. But to ensure her stay, Hades has tricked Persephone into eating seven pomegranate seeds. Zeus's compromise: Persephone will spend spring and summer and fall with her mother on earth and then descend to the underworld to be with her husband for the rest of the year.

Three quarters of the year is not a bad percentage, but it's all or nothing for Demeter. During her daughter's absence, she inflicts on the earth a short-term version of her earlier punishment. Call it winter.

Because I am entering the wintertime of my life as a woman and a writer, I identify with Demeter. I, too, want to be always producing, summertime year round. I am bereft without my writing, afraid to let go even for a short spell.

But I am also Persephone. That "beginner's mind" self who has to discover how to write each new book. A long journey she must embark on, again and again, taking risks, including separation from the safety of her mother, her accomplished work. Which is why Persephone swallows those pomegranate seeds. In order to flower she needs to keep returning to the underworld, where those seeds can germinate.

Hades is the character I least want to internalize. What writer doesn't dread those incoherent or silent spells? Terrifying and dangerous as the encounter can be—not every writer returns to tell the tale—we need his dark energy, Lorca's duende, Dylan Thomas's "force that through the green fuse drives the flower." Without it, the writing is tidy, lackluster, skimming the surface. It is not writing that can take us far, help us make meaning, provide string for the labyrinth of being a human being, especially an older human being.

Because I find myself in the underworld, I hold fast to the string of the Demeter-Persephone-Hades story. This story reminds me that my time in Hades will probably come to an end; that my Demeter will probably reunite with her Persephone; that deep inside me, I am carrying one of those pomegranate seeds.

2

My mother died in April 2012, within four months of my father's death. They were old (eighty-six and ninety-six), both afflicted with Alzheimer's. I had been losing them little by little for years. When the final loss came, I thought I would be ready. What I had not foreseen was that their daughter would die with them, and that she was a large part of the writer I had become.

Perhaps because ours is a Latino "we" culture, I always thought of myself as the writer, not *in* the family, but *of* the family. The compulsion for writing at all was to make meaning of our experience, in the belief that the story would hold us

together now that we had lost the context of our native country and culture. And so, I was blown away when my first novel
was met with intense family disapproval, particularly from
my mother, who accused me of betrayal for telling *our* stories
to *them*. "But it's fiction," I kept defending myself lamely. The
truer statement would have been: There is no *us* and *them*; we
become each other in the world of story.

My mother's furious reaction plunged me into a long, painful sojourn in the underworld. I thought I would never write
again. That should have been a clue that the writer and the
daughter were wedded as tightly together as Demeter and
Persephone.

But I found my voice again; I wrote a second novel. And I
attribute my endurance to the fact that by the time of my first
novel's publication, I was already an older writer, forty-one,
who'd been writing seriously since my undergraduate years.
I had also survived several decades in that underworld that
the culture then consigned "minority writers" to. As a woman,
a Latina, and an immigrant, I had been sent to the kitchen,
where I ate and grew strong in the company of Langston
Hughes, Maxine Hong Kingston, Leslie Marmon Silko, Gwen-
dolyn Brooks, and many other muses and mentors, some of
them white and male who had strayed from the company of
the front rooms (Yeats, Wordsworth, Blake, Roethke) to talk
to me (at any rate, their work spoke to me). The hardiness and
persistence developed over years of cultural disregard and disappointments allowed my older writing self to survive a familial reaction that might have crushed my younger writing self.

In her later years, my mother embraced my work. If my
books had been babies, they would have assumed pride of
place along with photos of her other grandchildren and great-

grandchildren. In fact, my mother commissioned a Dominican painter to copy an image of the Virgen de la Altagracia
from one of my children's books onto a back wall of their
property in Santiago, where my parents had returned to spend
their last years. The archbishop celebrated a mass in front of
the mural and declared the spot a national pilgrimage stop.
From banishment to enshrined—my mother's reactions were
always, like Demeter's, all or nothing.

The older writer has to bury the daughter who first set out
on the journey; whose childhood, horrid or idyllic or a mix
of both, provided the gasoline to get her out from under the
parental voiceover and into her own voice. She has survived so
many endings, including the endings of her books, the death
of the writer who wrote the last book, so that she can become
the writer who will write the next book; she should be adept
at spending these periodic and by now predictable sojourns
in the underworld. But death, if it means what it says, means
death. If she has the certainty that she will write again, then
call it a hiatus, call it research, call it a book tour, but it's not
the underworld.

Some writers never do come back from these silences,
just as some writers never get near their duendes, those little
deaths. I don't know if their fate is any better, because the writing dies, disconnected from this vital, composting stuff. It becomes the thing whereof many best sellers are made. Not a bad
fate, if you can be happy with that.

But I am my father's daughter, or was. He was heavily in-
vested in my work. Its intensity, its need to redeem our story.
He provided a lot of its fuel: his enormous need to prove himself worthy. My books proved it. He would call from a pay
phone on the street afraid to face my mother's ire, and I would

come home from a day of not writing in my office, a day in the underworld of silence, to his message on my answering machine: *Your mother will get over this. Don't give up hope. Keep writing.*

Good-bye to that gasoline.

3

The older writer has to find new fuel for the writing. Of course, she can just keep doing the writing out of the habit of writing. But it will show. The husk of a seed that does not germinate.

The public sources of fuel—fame, status, "love," money— she'd be lying if she said they are no longer enticing, especially in their older-writer equivalents: esteem, inclusion, affection, security. But they don't hold the same charge anymore. Either she has already gotten some of the above, or she knows that the roots that can nourish her in this next phase of life have to go deeper. Maybe the real work will now be shifting the focus, centering the soul in a larger ground of being. Who knows? The only way for her to find things out is by writing.

Meanwhile, the young ones are coming, the young ones are coming. There is relief in their arrival, for what writer who loves books would want all storytelling to end with her? *Après moi, le silence.* No way! Let the young ones have their turn.

But they arrive with such noise, albeit so smart and often brilliant, and with all their newfangled toys, their Internet, e-mails, blogs and tweets and liking on Facebook, so many new ways of telling their stories, ways the older writer needs their help to negotiate. And when she confesses that she'd much rather read a book with pages she can turn than a button to turn on, they turn on her and smile benignly or not so benignly, and she can see it in their eyes, tick-tock.

It is their turn. She has a different role to play now. It's her turn to listen to their Scheherazades, to write introductions to anthologies of writers under forty, to review first novels or blurb them, all the many ways of being an elder-statesman writer. An earlier generation—or some of the generous ones in that earlier generation—did these things for her.

With the years, as more of the people she loves and the parts of her that existed only in relation to them die off, she finds herself frequently in the underworld and for extended spells. It no longer feels seasonal, but like a place where she might have to learn how to live from now on. And if there is a pomegranate seed of promise here, it is the knowing that this world, too, needs to be storied.

*

MARGARET ATWOOD

ON CRAFT

One of my University Professors used to say, there's only one real question to be asked about any work, and that was: Is it alive, or dead? I happen to agree, but in what does this aliveness or deadness exist? The biological definition would be that living things grow and change and can have offspring whereas dead things are inert. In what ways can a text grow and have offspring? Only through interaction with a reader, no matter how far that reader may be from the writer in time and space.

MARGARET ATWOOD, *Negotiating with the Dead: A Writer on Writing*

It's a thrill to be here, it really is. So I say thank you for inviting me and hello to all my Twitter pals. And hello also to the members of the Margaret Atwood Society.

Now, the thing about a society is that you don't usually get

This essay was delivered as the keynote speech at the Association of Writers and Writing Programs conference in Chicago, February 2012.

one until you're dead. I am one of those people about whom other people are sometimes beginning to wonder. Because if you've taken somebody's work in, particularly, high school, you know they're dead. We had a curious experience at my house a few years ago—we were throwing a party for other writers in our province, and a lot of them had come, and it was a bit crowded. And you know writers: they get overexcited. One younger woman writer got overexcited and she thought she was having a heart attack just from being in my house. She wasn't really having a heart attack, she was having a ball of gas as big as a grapefruit, which was discovered later. But at the time she thought she was having a heart attack. So we took her into the living room and laid her down on the sofa and shooed everybody else out of the room. And Graeme did deep breathing with her and I called 911. And very shortly two huge strapping muscly young paramedics came galumphing up the steps. And they went in with their machines and shooed everybody out, and the following conversation took place:

FIRST PARAMEDIC: *Do you know whose house this is?*
SECOND PARAMEDIC: *No, whose house is it?*
FIRST PARAMEDIC: *This is Margaret Atwood's house.*
SECOND PARAMEDIC: *Margaret Atwood? Is she still alive?*

Well, some days I wonder.

The craft of writing, which is what I was asked to speak about—since I always do what I'm told—is what I will be speaking about. It is a great pleasure to be speaking about it with you today at such a gathering. And such a gathering it is. So many people interested in writing. And so many people teaching it. I feel a little like a voice from the tomb. Or at least a voice from the past, because when I began writing, writing was not taught. Or rather, what is now called "Creative Writing" was not taught. In high school we were expected to write essays, and we did write them—with attention paid to the rules of grammar, and half a mark off for each spelling mistake. I was not so good at spelling. I could handle words like *scrophulariaceae*, no problem, but fouled up regularly on words like *weird*—which I can only spell to this day by repeating "They are the three *weird* sisters; they are not the three *wired* sisters."

It was in high school that I proclaimed my intention of being a writer, causing some parental angst. "Well," said my mother, "if you're going to be a writer you'd better learn to spell."

"Others will do that for me," I replied rather loftily. And so it has proven to be. Whether those others be editors or spell check or the little red squiggly line that has its own opinions but is not always right, or that mythical entity of days of yore, Bob the paperclip. I never actually saw Bob the paperclip—he graced the computers of others, though he never manifested himself to me. Instead I got the little box. The little box that did somersaults and said helpfully, "Are you trying to write a letter?" But I heard about Bob the paperclip, which is how I know he is a mythical entity. The moral of this story: if you want to be a writer, spelling is the least of your worries.

I was sixteen then. Where was the AWP when I needed it? All I had was a lone magazine called *Writer's Market*. It was through *Writer's Market* that I learned about the typed self-addressed stamped envelope and about putting your name at the top of every page. This was in the days when pages were made of paper and could therefore get lost. And I also learned in *Writer's Market* that the things that paid the most per word were stories in true romance magazines. There were no work-shops on how to write stories for true romance magazines, but I decided—and I did decide this, briefly—that I would write stories for true romance magazines in order to make my living, and then in the evenings I would write my works of staggering literary genius. And I felt that it should not be too hard to write stories for true romance magazines, because I bought several of these and read them, and the plots seemed to be reducible to a fairly simple set of propositions: Girl falls in love with Wrong Boy. Right Boy is there, but Right Boy works boringly in a shoe store. Wrong Boy has a motorcycle. You can tell already that this is the plot of *Wuthering Heights*. Something then happens on the sofa—this is the fifties, remember, the age of Playtex all-rubber panty girdles—something happens on the sofa, which is delineated as "And then we were one. Dot dot dot dot dot dot dot."

So I could do the plots very well, but I could not do the dots. There was some trick to it that I never mastered. So instead of doing that, I went off to study English at University. When I got to University, creative writing was still not taught, or not formally. In the fourth year of honors English, you could, if so disposed, join something called "English for Zero," for which you did not get credit. But you could sit in a circle and read your poems out loud to the four other people in the group. Which I did. Extracurricularly, you could join the staff of the college magazine, which published reviews, drawings, stories, and poetry. And you could write all those things, plus do the drawings, under different names, to make the magazine look full. Which I also did. This was 1961—not a high-point year for those interested in writing at the University of Toronto, not noted then for the arts. The writer Wyndham Lewis lived in Toronto a decade or so before that time, and when he was at a party a society matron asked him where he was living. He told her. She said, "Mr. Lewis, that is not a very fashionable address." To which he replied, "Madam, Toronto is not a very fashionable address." Nor was it, then.

Even more extracurricularly, you could put on your scratchy turtleneck sweater and read your poetry at a coffeehouse called the Bohemian Embassy on Poetry Nights, which were Tuesdays. Other things went on, on other, presumably more exciting, nights. That was more like the real thing. They had an espresso machine, the first one anybody in Toronto had ever seen, which was worshipped like a god.

All of which is to say that I am in no way formally prepared to give a talk called "The Craft of Writing," because I never studied the craft of writing in any formal way. I did it the way one did it then: I read and wrote and read and wrote and read and wrote and ripped up and crossed out and started again. Which is pretty much what still happens. I am surprised by people who say that they want to write but turn out not to like reading. Those people don't want to write, not really. They want an audience to sit down beside them and hear their sad story, and that's about the end of it. They'd be happier on reality TV, because it's much less work.

There, I used the W-word. And I'm not afraid to use it again. Work. Because craft has to do with work, whereas art is what you may get as a result of the craft. "The life so short, the craft so long to learn," said Chaucer. "The Arts and Crafts movement," said the early twentieth century. "In my craft and sullen art," said Dylan Thomas. Art. Craft. Not the same, it seems. But what's the difference? Well, one word is fashionable at the moment and the other is not. Words come and go like lipstick colors. "Art" was doing well around the middle of the twentieth century; "craft" was not. If you were interested in art, then you might attract a derisive term: "artsy-fartsy." But no one spoke of "craftsy-waftsies." I bet certain university faculties would get more funding right now if they renamed themselves the faculty of crafts in lieu of the faculty of arts.

There is an instinctive feeling right now, *art* implies elitist—eek, we can't have that—and possibly even dilettante or aesthete. Whereas *craft*, that has a more solid, proletarian feel to it. Craft has dirt under its fingernails. Craft isn't something you *are*, as in "artistic genius." It's something you do—you can learn it.

So, in respect to writing, what can you learn? What can be learned, and thus taught?

Art comes from an old Greek root, meaning "joint." This is the kind you can't inhale. Something with a hinge. Something, therefore, with several parts. Related to this word are *arthritis*, a disease of the joints; *arthropod*, jointed foot; *arm*; *armor*; *articulate*; *artisan*; and many others. Art is something man makes or puts together, as opposed to nature, which grows of itself. However, it may be true also that art is *human* nature, that it too grows by itself in a way. Art, or the templates upon which art is based, comes built in. Every young child picks up language, can understand narratives at a very early age, sings and dances, and makes images if given the wherewithal.

Then there's craft. *Craft* comes fairly directly from the Old English word "cræft," meaning primarily "physical strength," but by extension skill, knowledge, and the like. It's related to the German word *kraft* with a *k*, meaning "strength," which puts a whole new spin on Kraft Dinner. To have a craft is to have a strength and also a know-how, to understand how a thing is done, and to have the energy to carry it through. Even if you have talent, a gift, something that comes to you as an extra without work—even if you are gifted, you will not develop that gift unless you get down and dirty, what with the blacksmith's hammer and all. For your craft knowledge is your tool kit. It gives you the tools to put something together from its parts, so that it becomes articulate, so that it's many-footed, so that it might turn into art.

A word about tools. I grew up with tools, surrounded by tools. These were hand tools. We lived in the woods: there was no electricity, and besides, electric drills and screwdrivers and the like had not yet been invented. We needed the tools in order to make things, fix things, and demolish things. A demolished thing could be used for parts, to be incorporated into different things—and you can do the same with your writing. Cut when necessary, but don't throw out. Maybe you can use those parts later. There is nothing so satisfying as the right tool for the right job. There is nothing so frustrating as the wrong tool—or, worse, a tool in bad repair. Tools are kept shiny by use. If you want to slit a throat effectively, in art as well as in life, first sharpen the knife.

Here are some writing tools that are good to have handy in your tool kit.

The key signature. The key signature is the tone of your work. Is this work written in a major key, or in a minor key? Is it light, or is it dark? Or is it sort of beige? If so, is that the tone you intended?

Tempo. How fast are we moving? Vary the tempo. Otherwise things can get monotonous.

Voice. Who is speaking, and to whom? Where does the speaker stand in relation to the listener, namely, the reader?

Does the speaker know more than we do, to reveal it little by little? Does the speaker know less than we do, the poor fool, in which case we can see it coming—don't open that door!— but she can't? How much would the speaker be able to know, given her situation?

The difference between plot and structure. The plot is the sequence of events viewed lineally: this happened, and then this, and then this. The structure is the order in which you tell that story. The sequence of events leading to and through the Trojan War is the plot of the *Iliad*. The structure begins in the middle, with Achilles sulking in his tent, and goes both backward and forward from there.

A word about writer's blocks. Most blocks in the writing of novels are either blocks of voice or blocks of structure. For voice blocks, change the narrator or the tense. See if that works. For structure blocks, change the first scene, the point of insertion. See if that works. If none of this works, go to the movies. And remember Charles Dickens, who said, "Make them laugh; make them cry; make them wait."

Finally, a word on another word. That word is *crafty*. This word once meant "skilled," but even by the twelfth century, it was taking on its modern meaning of cunning or sly or devious or too clever by half. How does this fit in with your tool kit? Well, sometimes a bag of tools is also a bag of tricks, like a magician's tricks, and sometimes those tools are used for devious purposes, such as deceptions. Writers are, among everything else, illusionists, and some of the tools of craft are tools of illusion. For instance, we talk about the writer's voice, but it isn't the writer's voice the reader actually hears. It's his or her own voice, tricked into doing an impersonation. Writers, if they've been at it long enough, come to know this about themselves and what they do: they are not always nice people. They know too much. But they are, on some level, crafty people. They hide things. They stage ambushes. They keep one hand in their pocket. They carry concealed weapons. They plan surprises. They have a certain orneriness, a stubbornness. If they fall off the horse, they get back on. They know the story is endless. They know the story is human, and defines that word, *human*. They know the story they are telling is part of that ancient human thread. It leads way back. With their help, it will also lead forward.

So spin those yarns, all you skillful tale-tellers of the world, with all the art and all the craft you may command. Alive or dead, we'll be listening.

MADELEINE BLAIS

THE RATIO IS NARROWING

I am part of a band of women who graduated from college in the late sixties who chose to pursue their literary destinies by working at newspapers. We were English majors who wanted to change the world and have an adventure to boot. We came of age at a time of tumult: civil rights demonstration, the war in Vietnam, the emerging women's and gay rights movements. We inhabited a world in which reality had outstripped the imagination as a source of the outlandish.

When I say we were not always encouraged in our ambition, I mean it, and I have as proof a letter sent to a friend who applied in 1967 to the Internship Scholarship Program run by the Newspaper Fund. The letter was signed by the executive director Paul Swensson, dated December 20, 1967:

> Unfortunately, I cannot submit your application to the directors for their approval. Their program is open only to young men. Let me explain.

Since the start of this decade there has been a shortage of young men in the newsroom. The Newspaper Fund reacted by offering scholarships to interested students on liberal arts campuses where little or no formal education in journalism is available. It helps interested young men find summer reporting jobs; upon completion of a successful season of work, it grants a $500 scholarship to be applied to the senior year tuition bill.

In the broad field of journalism, there are many opportunities for both young men and women. But there is no shortage of young women seeking newspaper jobs. The supply in some areas exceeds the demands of editors. The ratio of women in the newsroom is about one to every three men. The ratio is narrowing.

At the time it was sent, the letter was legal, the discrimination acceptable.

Reading it now, across the vale of time, I feel a pang of guilt-ridden gratitude: I am so glad that letter went to someone else and not to me, because I am sure it would have stopped me in my tracks.

I wound up in the newspaper business in a roundabout way.

I had always dreamed of celebrity, or, if not celebrity, something akin to it. I fantasized being part of some larger, well-recognized narrative. In the small town where I grew up, nothing much happened beyond the slow accumulation of seconds and minutes and hours: we embodied Thornton Wilder's already slow-paced *Our Town*, but on downers. A cow ate some rotten apples. The sap in March should be plentiful. The crocuses are late this year.

I longed for action.

I craved some kind of newsworthy event, international, seedy, spectacular: it did not matter. I wanted to find Russian spies cowering in the field behind my house, or watch as the lunch counter owner up the street got arrested for something connected to his love of dirty jokes and girlie magazines, or duck while a B-52 from nearby Westover Air Force Base swooped across the sky, flat-hatting over the town common. Other children dreamt of time travel in a princess outfit or riding a horse at full speed across a windswept prairie. I conjured images of *Life* magazine coming to town.

When I was ten, I spent a few weeks at a Girl Scout camp where a woman interviewed me and other campers for a feature story in the *Holyoke Daily Transcript & Telegram*. I observed her with curiosity: the superior way in which she tottered around camp in high heels, the slash of red lipstick showing she meant business, the rustle of the pages of her notebook as she saturated them with squiggles. Her manner, both secretarial and commanding, took my breath away. She was like a times table, worthy of being memorized.

Her version of Camp Sandy Brook claimed almost an entire page of the newspaper. It was a diva of an article, grand and overbearing. Under her expansive gaze, s'mores and a campfire took on operatic intensity.

She quoted me as loving *everything*, including soft scrambled eggs, an exaggeration that I was powerless to rebut. The story distorted my level of enthusiasm to the point that even the most sensible person might be inclined to believe that the ghost of Juliette Gordon Low, the founder of the Girl Scouts, a paragon who grappled with a philandering husband, deafness, back problems, and cancer, and who was eventually buried in full uniform, had returned to life and taken up residence in an otherwise unremarkable creature, me.

I was elated when the article appeared, convinced that my life would change in some fundamental way as a result of this attention. It did not, but I could not shake the image of that reporter, how sleek she looked, how self-contained, with her notebook and her pencil and her penetrating gaze. Maybe that could be me some day, establishing a connection with a story larger than my own, even if the connection is a tenuous one, swaying on the rickety rope bridge of a byline.

The first time I openly confessed my desire to go into journalism and to become a writer out loud was in the summer I was seventeen, right before leaving for college in 1965. I had just encountered my second journalist at a neighbor's cocktail party, which I attended, probably none too willingly, with my mother. One of the guests was a middle-aged editor from the *Springfield Union*. Although I knew plenty of people with jobs—such as a teacher who left for school every day hoping that her unemployed husband would find his own work (he never did), a man with a plumbing and electrical supply business, a shoe store manager, a postmistress, the pharmacist in the center of town who kept track of everyone's medical secrets and didn't mind sharing them, even a dentist who treated nuns for free, clearly banking on days off purgatory—I had never met an editor before.

He had only one question for me.

The question was not: "What papers do you read?" or "What journalists do you admire?" or "Do you have any idea of the things you would like to cover?"

He gave me a once-over and then rubbed the cold rim of his glass with an index finger. "I wonder if you're tough enough."

Frown. "You don't look it."

"Are you," he asked, "a virgin?"

I was twice horrified, not just at the question, but also that my mother was within earshot.

My mother could not always be counted on to meet her six children's needs due to the simple numerical reality of how many there were of us and how few of her. But on the occasion of this assault on my presumed virtue, she went into a full-court press. Before I knew it, the man was chasing after me, holding his drink aloft, shouting, "Are you a virgin?" He was followed by my mother, chasing after him, holding her drink aloft, admonishing, "You have no right to ask her that." I managed to elude them both and spill out of the house into the yard, using the lightness of my youth against them, aware that whether I said yes, appeasing my mother as to my enduring wholesomeness, or whether I said no, demonstrating to the editor he was incorrect about my fatal lack of worldliness, there would always be one wrong answer.

In the spring of my junior year, at my small Catholic women's college, I was elected to be the editor of the four-page weekly newspaper. As the editor, I got to go far afield to conferences for college newspaper editors, such as to Valparaiso College in Indiana, in the summer of 1968. The other student editors were enraged by the Soviet tanks plowing down protestors in what is now the Czech Republic. I experienced this entire historical uprising with the narrow view of someone who is freshly hatched. How worldly my peers seemed to me, how global: if only I could be informed and debonair, like them, and care about something that far away. Later I went to Washington, DC, to the Shoreham Hotel where Buckminster Fuller and Muhammad Ali put in appearances and made themselves available for interviews with us: *Us!* a bunch of striving young baby boomers.

At one or the other of those conferences I saw a flyer for the Columbia Graduate School of Journalism and decided to send off for an application. It said the school accepted 110 students, ten from foreign countries and ten women. Among the requirements was a recommendation from a professional journalist. The only one I knew was the "Are you a virgin?" guy, and by then I was not so naïve as to think contacting him would be a smart move.

The person who came to the rescue was some kid I hardly knew, the boyfriend of a girl in my Latin class who took my dilemma on as his own and suggested we drive to the nearby suburb of Larchmont one bright winter's Saturday morning. We went in his beat-up car to the old neighborhood where he grew up, because the man who lived in the house next door used to work for *Newsweek* and maybe he still did. This scheme felt thin and shallow, and it did not occur to me that the man might not even answer the door, although it should have. This was at a time when all young people were considered hippies, and all hippies were considered dangerous, dirty, pot-smoking followers of iffy gurus (Timothy Leary and Charles Manson being among the most notorious examples). The generational divide was so strong that I had male friends who were not allowed by their fathers to join the rest of their families at the dining room table simply on the basis of the length of their hair.

We were lucky.

The man answered the door, recognized the boy, invited us in, and soon the two of them were catching up on mutual family gossip.

In time, I was called upon to explain my predicament.

I said I wanted to apply to grad school but I needed a recommendation from a professional journalist and I didn't really know any. I told him about the paper at my college and how much I enjoyed working on it and about the conferences I had gone to. He asked me questions, polite questions which struck me, given my previous experience, as disconcerting, such as "What papers do you read?" "What journalists do you admire?" and "Do you have any idea of the kinds of stories that you would like to cover?"

Finally, he said, "Sure, I'll write one for you."

And he did. (I have forgotten his name, but thank you, whoever, wherever, you are.)

Going from my sheltered background to a big university in a huge city was like being on 78 rpms for cultural growth. I had never heard of Yom Kippur. Initially, I thought it was the name of a professor from some foreign country I had never heard of, though I did not mind getting the day off on his account. At Columbia, I first heard of James Agee and Lillian Ross and George Orwell—from my better-read classmates. At Columbia, I had a professor, Paul Brodeur, who wrote articles for the *New Yorker*. The *New Yorker*: the very magazine that published *Hiroshima* and *In Cold Blood* in their entirety. I was in school the year that Joe McGinniss's *The $elling of the President* came out. McGinniss was only twenty-six years old, the youngest person ever to be on the *New York Times* best-seller list. How could someone that young be so successful? My classmates and I devoured his work with jealousy and despair.

My job interviews at newspapers were miserable exchanges in which a put-out-to-pasture former newsman was reduced to fending off eager young people while engaging in sports metaphors, usually involving balls in the outfield, as he outlined a vast empty expanse—my future.

Yet my already ink-stained heart remained set on working for a paper. The breakthrough came when I was hired as a suburban correspondent for the *Boston Globe* (no benefits, long hours, lousy beat, but a job is a job). My duties entailed going to night meetings in Quincy, Braintree, Weymouth, and sometimes Milton while middle-aged civic-minded adults decided whether or not to increase the tax base in their towns or to start a neighborhood crime watch with occasional furloughs to cover other stories. Twice, I had assignments I now look back on and cringe. My male editors thought it would be amusing if I went underground and pretended to be a stewardess on several cross-country flights for TWA and also to be an escort for a new business that provided company for men from out of town. The first story wasn't so bad, though I must question the lax standards, even before 9-11, that allowed me to wear a flight attendant's real uniform without any training for emergencies. There was a sexist ad campaign for airlines popular at the time: a photo of a pretty stewardess with the legend, "I'm so and so. Fly me," whose cadences I cringe to admit I copied for my story: "I'm Madeleine. You could have flown me." The second was more pathetic: a man from Oklahoma City, hoping for a fun night in Bean Town, had to contend with me, who had a different goal, mocking him in print (my editors showed him one mercy: he remained anonymous.) Leering assignments were popular at the time: the famed feminist Gloria Steinem got an early break by pretending to be a Playboy bunny. Both of my assignments, with their gloss of forced fun, were humiliating, for me and also for the editors who thought they were a good idea in the first place.

Finally, a full-time job with benefits, in New Jersey at the *Trenton Times* as a feature writer, covering society in Trenton, including Easter egg hunts at the local Y, a Polish debutante ball, and an interview with a Jehovah's Witness to see if it was the end of the world after the region had been besieged by flood, fire, and drought. (He told me, solemnly, "The Bible doesn't even mention Trenton.")

My last major story before quitting the paper was the 1976 Democratic Convention in New York City in which Jimmy Carter won the nomination. The trip into the city was a cheap date for the *Trenton Times*: it was only an hour or so away by train, so a whole gang of us were rotated in and out, feeling that borrowed glow that comes from a brush with history.

I could not have been happier: a choice assignment at last, an assignment that signified, a *guy* assignment. Whatever I wrote would begin with the dateline NEW YORK CITY. Could there be more prestige, more pizzazz?

If the 1970s embodied rampant mediocrity in the rest of the country, it marked a nadir for New York City, when crime spiraled in one direction, up, and basic civility spiraled in an equal but opposite direction, down. The area outside Madison Square Garden was a breeding ground for luckless lost souls with nothing left to lose: curbside philosophers such as the man who stood on one corner every day, all day, carrying a sign indicating that victory was nigh. He possessed the kind of dense, matted, and extensive beard that contains, one assumes, not only crumbs, but also, possibly, critters. The victory to which he referred could have been for anything from a game of tiddlywinks to the clash of enemies at the end of the world.

He was gone from his usual perch during the week of the convention. Gone, also, the lady with the beard, and her pal who wore a dozen coats no matter what the weather, the man with the shopping cart filled with newspapers and rolled-up balls of tinfoil and single shoes and assorted other treasures of a dubious ilk, and the guy who liked to quote the Bible, especially the more lurid passages, threatening hellfire and disfigurement and parasites that eat you from the inside out. Disappeared, all of them, for the time being. With all those bigwigs, conventioneers, and media types coming to town, the police arrested anyone whose appearance or behavior might be construed as offensive on charges of vagrancy or of being a public nuisance.

As we reporters entered Madison Square Garden, with its red, white, and blue bunting and streamers and balloons, the delegates, all boozed up, sang *Happy Days Are Here Again* at the top of their lungs. I took in the crowd of thousands and realized that I was in over my head. How among the multitude do you find the singular story and tell it in a singular way? The more nervous I got, the weaker my reporting became, so that by the end of the week I was writing gibberish.

On the last day of covering the convention, I was assigned to write about the Garden after it had cleared out, when the delegates had all left for good. Phones were dismantled, pamphlets and pennants put in the trash, chairs folded for storage. I had no trouble writing this story, because at last I had something to say and I felt a surge of emotion, in this case, pure relief.

NEW YORK —— To end with the ending:

New York City outside Madison Square Garden, in the heart of this sleepless heap of concrete and asphalt, a neon night only ninety minutes after the final evening of the Democratic Convention. . . . The last button vendor is packing his wares; the abortion foes are home in bed. Gone, too, are the lovers of Jesus. Away, for the first time in four days, are the people who want to terminate the police state or get 40 hours pay for 30 hours work or elect Nobody for President or legalize cocaine.

The cabs are back cruising the streets, not waiting expectantly, a yellow sea, outside the convention. The drivers will return to weather as a topic; no more tip-tailored spiels about how Gerald Ford is a good guy couldn't be nicer, but he's pasta without the tomato sauce and the country needs some spice.

Inside the Garden, to reverse Bob Dylan's phrase, it is a place busy dying, not busy being born. Dying will take a whole week; this is no ordinary circus tent.

Jimmy Carter is a prophet. Two hours ago, surrounded by thousands, accepting his party's nomination for the Presidency, he said he sees an America on the move again. And he was right. There they are after Carter is gone, Americans on the move, two hundred laborers, electricians, carpenters, and trash collectors, the men who will sweep up after history.

An electrician piling dozens of phones in brown bags marked rubbish asks a friend to guard the phones while he rustles up a dolly. He says the convention has taught him something; he says it has taught him there are petty thieves in all 50 states.

The last night, finally, was a turn-on, a buzz, a Grits-Fritz blitz. They even threw a couple of beach balls. There were lots, as they say in Baptist circles, of joyful noises.

But now, at an hour and a half after the midnight hour, the cake and the circus and the 3,000 telephones and the beach balls are gone, like the leaves in autumn, vanished. The $2.2 million worth of security has dwindled to a few cops on the beat. The derelicts and the whores can come home now, if they want.

Hail, hail, the gang's all gone.

Yet I cannot summon those words without cringing.

I actually called all those cabs "a yellow sea?"

Someone, tell me this is a typo.

And I am incredulous: only $2.2 million worth of security?

But I did learn something about my own mindset as a reporter.

Covering the party *after* it was over helped me to crystallize my thoughts about which stories I wanted to tell, and which I did not.

I recognized the stories that most attracted me as the ones everyone else had abandoned.

The derelicts and the whores can come home now, if they want.

Eight weeks later, I would be on the road to Miami, where I would eventually work for *Tropic Magazine* at the *Miami Herald*. And that is where, thanks to a battalion of nurturing editors, male and female, and to a town where stories grow on trees like mangoes and cocoanuts, I found my voice.

And so began my time on the staff, specializing in writing about outsiders, people who teeter on the edge, without a safety net.

I covered old people losing their homes, dismayed at the developers who sought to move them elsewhere. I took a Spanish immersion class offered by the county. I wrote about a twelve-year-old who killed his mother and his brother, sparing himself and his father at the last minute. A teenaged babysitter who smothered five infants to death up in the Panhandle. A teenaged prostitute with AIDS who had no qualms about infecting her clients. I covered a day care center that got closed down thanks to allegations of molestation *and* satanic rituals. When I first outlined the story to an editor, he said, "Both charges? Isn't that, like, a little greedy? (Newsroom humor.) I spent weeks on end gathering information about the famed Fontainebleau after it got a facelift. I covered a brilliant teacher and her fourth-grade classroom in Liberty City in which almost all the windows were boarded up and every morning yielded a fresh crop of syringes in the playground. I spent so much time trying to capture the mood and methods at a psychiatric crisis center at Jackson Memorial Hospital that the staff became concerned for my welfare and worried that I was delusional, my principal fantasy being that I *thought* I was writing a story for the *Herald* when I was not. I interviewed Hannah Kahn, a poet whose daughter with Down Syndrome had been her greatest creation. In one of those quotes that I invoke in my head all the time, Hannah told me, "I like my life; sometimes I don't like the facts of my life." She also said that in the first wave of grief, when she finally acknowledged her daughter's deficits and played out in her mind what they might mean in the long run, the coffee she drank tasted terrible, tasted "like blood." I profiled a young boxer named Elvis Yerro whose promise was short-lived. I flew all the way to Mexico in pursuit of the birth mother of a little five-year-old girl named Cindy who appeared to have been illegally adopted. When the story ran and the *Herald* didn't even bother to mention my international travel as part of the promo, my editor said, "That just shows you how classy the *Herald* is."

I look back on my career from the safe perch of the present and marvel at my luck, knowing that women before me hacked their way through the jungle to clear a path for others who would, like me, have an easier time. Not only was I able to earn my living as a writer, I was able to earn my living as a teacher of writing. What could be thriftier than getting paid to do what you love in two different ways?

Plenty of young women I knew defaulted on their dreams. A career in journalism or in writing is not for the faint of heart. You have to believe against all evidence to the contrary that the world needs you to mine your past for a memoir or to cover its events—to tell the story of a team or of a child killer or of an aging playwright down on his luck—and that the world just does not know it. Your job is to bridge the gap between your ambition and not just universal indifference, but also at times huge roadblocks. This is not new.

But at least now women who choose my line of work are not the exception. I hesitate to tell this to Mr. Swensson of the Newspaper Fund lest it go to his head: but he was right. The ratio is narrowing.

✳
ROSELLEN BROWN

PARSING AMBITION

Every Sunday, like so many who are still addicted to paper, I sit at the kitchen table and turn to the *New York Times Book Review,* whose attention, for better or worse, is a measure of a certain kind of public notice. I used to find myself idly thinking, as writers will, "Oh, wouldn't it be lovely to have your book featured on the cover of the *Book Review*?"

And then I'd stop myself and, with that temple-bopping gesture from the old TV ad for fancied-up tomato juice ("I could have had a V-8!"), I would be forced to remember that I *have* had a book featured on the cover of the *Book Review.* I am not boasting; being reviewed so prominently is as much a matter of luck and marketing as it is of talent, as witness all the wonderful books that are born to blush unseen on the tables at the Strand bookstore, where reviewers cadge a little money for their unread copies. On the contrary, I have come to terms with the fact that, for whatever reason we drink from this sweet and bitter cup called writerly ambition, and no matter how, at its best, it should quench our thirst, *it will not sat-*

isfy us. Our ego needs are deep—unassuageable—or we could never have done this difficult thing, and done it for so long; we wouldn't have found it worth the dangers.

But what, in fact, is that "writerly ambition" about? And is it a constant over time?

Many years ago I had a dream so potent I've never forgotten it. I tend to interpret my nocturnal wanderings in the most obvious and conventional ways, but this dream didn't worry me as much as it amused me for the dramatic way it posed a foundational question.

When I was in college I was at first a contributor to, and then the editor of, our campus literary magazine, called *Focus*. I was writing only poetry back then, earnestly, wearing the requisite black and taking myself very seriously indeed; the only writerly accessory I lacked was a cigarette habit, for which I'll be eternally grateful. On the day we brought the finished magazine from the printer's, we would put large boxes of *Focus* out on a table at the crossroads of the campus, Barnard Hall, so that students and faculty could pick them up as they passed. And I was accustomed to receiving comments on—read *praise for*—my writing. Sometimes a faculty member would even be kind enough to send a letter of appreciation for one of my poems, and you can imagine how I cherished those, and how much of what little confidence I had was bolstered by, even built on, such small local fame.

And here's the very simple dream which I think I had while I was still at Barnard, or perhaps soon after. On the day the boxes of *Focus* arrived, I stood behind a pillar invisibly watching the passing crowd as it picked up the magazine, presumably preparing to gloat, until I realized that I—or we, the staff—had forgotten to affix my name to my poem. And in the dream the question was clear to me: Did that matter? *Should* that matter? Wasn't it enough that the poem was read and maybe appreciated for its own sake? Or did it only have value if I could take credit for it, as coin of my realm?

Was this about me and my social standing—such as it was—or did I truly, as I hoped in my sober moments, want nothing more than to think the work's quality would allow it to dwell in some small corner of the world of literature, not my personal kingdom of ego gratification?

What, in other words, were the uses of ambition? What *should* they be? What was craft for, or any kind of longing to do something well? To make something *fine*: Was *that* ambition? Did everything well done need public acclamation, and, if not, in whose name was it offered, and to whom? And then, was language different from other "made things" because without a listener to receive it, it became that most famous of all trees, the one that falls in the deserted forest? Eudora Welty said she wrote for the "it" that inheres in the pleasure of *doing* the work itself and not in the adulation that might follow it. In one of her poems, Marge Piercy says that better than I can: "Work is its own cure. You have to / like it better than being loved."

My friend Lucia is multitalented: she weaves, she knits, she creates incomparable ceramics; she used to make welded sculpture; she wrote and drew delightful books for children. But never once did she feel the need to "go public" with any of that (except that she used the books when she was a teacher, and now she does clay work with children). "Why don't you show the pieces you've welded," I would ask, perplexed, "these beautiful coats you've sewn out of fabric you've woven? Why don't you publish the books?"

"Why?" she would challenge in return.

"Why?" I would echo. "Why not?"

"Isn't it enough that making them gives me pleasure? Why do I need anybody else to approve of them?"

I have never had a satisfactory response. This is not art for art's sake; it is making for making's sake.

Kipling advised, in an acid remark that makes more and more sense to me, "Beware the twin imposters success and failure." These days, I find that acknowledgment something of a relief. I have many published words behind me, and many jobs they have, incidentally and after the fact, secured for me. Being free—or freer—of the temptation to be preoccupied by questions of reputation is a little like the way so many postmenopausal women are pleasantly surprised to discover that sex has a new piquancy once it's not shadowed by the dangers of pregnancy and the exhaustion of early motherhood. There's a certain unanticipated delight at such freedom from consequences, and a chance to concentrate on essences, not appearances.

But no one would pretend there aren't losses, and for us, we of a certain age, there's the sense that we're running out of time to write our Platonic ideal of a book. And, much as we recognize its inevitability, it still shocks us to feel the hot breath of our successors on our not-so-firm necks. The farther those successors disappear into the forest of technology—publishing online, Blackberrying, Facebooking and blogging and texting and tweeting in what must be a forty-eight-hour day to accommodate all that communication and hasty opinion—the more I find my hopeless, helpless self returned, pen in hand, to the thing itself, not hors de combat but hors de competitiveness. However hard we work at learning how to manage the new machines, my generation will always be immigrants in a land our successors were born into. (Note to self: it's all over if you ever use the word *newfangled*.)

It follows that one of these days we will have more trouble than we already do attracting publishers devoted to the flavor of the month—it's a lot more satisfying to take a chance on a new (preferably photogenic) writer with no midlist track record—but we can still speak to each other, and I think we listen with a bit more patience, a bit more focus than the children who can type so fast with their thumbs. At least I know that every woman of a certain age to whom I've mentioned that I'm writing a book of stories to be called *Late Loves* has promised to buy a copy!

> . . . each time
> something happens that we have always expected—
> events tolling like bells, never quite surprising—
> what can I think of but the final
> stone to come, the day they tell us will also arrive,
> sooner, later, but no way not arrive? They haven't lied
> yet—we'd better believe them.

I am forcing myself to forgive the narcissism of quoting from myself (in the guise of my "character" Cora Fry) to acknowledge the inescapable. True, too true, they haven't lied yet, those threatening voices. Dante was an innocent: We *do* know how many death has undone.

But what they can't tell us is how that death will approach and take us, suddenly or slowly, in a single garroting or a slow dwindling or . . . the variations, we know, are as endless as they are unpredictable. Nor does it help to recognize that we have been dying piecemeal all our lives, or at least since our so-called physical peak so many decades ago.

No news in any of that, but what's begun to be hard is the impossibility of knowing the speed and depth of our losses. All of us joke about incipient Alzheimer's. Every time we misplace our keys or forget a name, not to mention an appointment, we say, with a cheerfulness that surely masks a depth of genuine terror, that maybe we've got a touch of one kind of dementia or another. So we whistle past the graveyard but keep on walking.

My father, in his late eighties, would try to play the delightful, thumping ragtime and marches I grew up loving—my brothers and I used to high-step around the piano to a piece we called "the big noise"—and fall into despair when his fingers just couldn't do it any more. The wrong notes and collapsed thumbs told the whole story of decline. We heard it and mourned. The beautiful actress whose face either records the passage of time or tries to outwit it with salves or surgery, the athlete whose legs are gone—the wreckage is visible, painful, public.

But for a writer who presumably lives by her wits the fear has an added dimension, and it isn't only her diminished powers. Because the losses are invisible, insidious, and (is this better or worse?) inconsistent, I am left wondering who will tell me when I have become as boring as Wordsworth when he'd outlived his glory. Who will dare suggest that my ideas are not sustainable, that my forward moves will turn out to be dead ends, and even my concerns look, to a fresher eye, outdated? What, to put it cruelly, is the accretion of wisdom and what the barnacles that adhere to an aging hulk?

Well, you may say, if the work is bad no one will publish it and then you'll know. Simple: let the marketplace bear the bad tidings. But what gets published is a notoriously unreliable guide to quality; we all hoard stories of the twenty-four rejections of this week's best seller, the self-published prize winner, all those gorgeous repudiations of the judgment of the so-called pros. Is anything more capricious than the fate of literary (or any artistic) accomplishment? Leaning on the public's reception of our work is dangerous because it can mislead us, for better or worse, just when our confidence has grown shaky and our output has slowed. Could it really be that, even with small children to raise, I published three books in three years?

A young friend of mine told me the other day that one of the things her publisher values is the "regularity" of her production, as if writing fiction were the result of a daily dose of prunes. She was more appalled by the word than by the expectation but, twenty-some years younger than I, she'll do it; at my age I'd no sooner promise a book every couple of years than climb Everest. Like my hair, my ideas are thinning.

These days, instead of those stories about the many-times-rejected books or the terribly reviewed works that became classics, what I find myself shamelessly collecting are the examples of people my age and older who have continued to be productive. The novelist Nicholas Delbanco has published a book called *Lastingness* that flies in the face of my qualms and anticipatory decrepitude: It is a compendium of stories about aging artists—writers, musicians, painters—who persevered not blindly but without wasting much time feeling their pulses to see if they were slowing. I've always hated the cheerleading of books like *Jews in Sports* or *Ten Who Beat the Odds*, because they only prove the rule by teasing out the exceptions. Perversely, all that the stories about how seventy is the new sixty and sixty the new fifty manage to do is call even greater attention to the saliency of age in our current culture. "Look!" they seem to say. "A lucky few seem impervious to expectations of decline. Aren't they wonderful!" But I have to admit that Delbanco's octo- and nonagenarians are a corrective to discouragement: These are the people who loved work more than being loved, who simply could not stop.

In his closing pages, Delbanco quotes a letter from John Updike that represents the long view and a refusal to indulge in anticipatory mourning:

> My own continuing to write at the age of three score and fifteen is a matter of genetics, long habit, and concrete aspirations. I set out to make a living with my pen, in privacy, in the commercial literary world as it existed, and am grateful that I managed. It's been a privilege and a pleasure, and it goes without saying that I've been lucky. No impairing disease. No war I was asked to help fight. No stupefying poverty yet no family wealth or business to limit my freedom. Lovely bright loving parents,

> then good loyal women and healthy children living with
> me. . . . A world where books were a common currency
> of an enlightened citizenry. Who wouldn't, thus condi-
> tioned, want to keep writing forever, and try to make
> books that deserve to last?

Parsing this paragraph can only remind us of how much its very language speaks from the past, and how some of it might rankle us as women and small-d democrats who are suspicious of what "an enlightened citizenry" can often mean up close. But still, similarly grateful, I honor his level-headed and undramatic reckoning that what is taken away can never fully subtract from what we have been given.

I was struggling with a book, wondering if I'd finish it before it finished me. Once upon a time a bad project was only a bad project; now I worry that my judgment is slipping, and my capacity to generate workable ideas. Eager to be encouraging, my husband said, "Well, would it really matter if you didn't publish another one? You've earned some relaxation. You can be proud of what you've done." He meant that, of course, as a kind of comfort, a few strokes of the hair I was so furiously tearing out. But, however well-intentioned, it was a knife to the heart. Obviously he's right, but if I don't push that stone uphill, what will I do? Who will I be?

I remonstrate with myself: Shouldn't I be past that narrow definition of myself and my worth by now? Of course, of course I should. But what was once the need to be praised and valued by others has, I recognize, begun to be reflexive; the question I posed to myself in that old dream is being answered by default: It's a measure of self-respect under the shadow of what I'm no longer sure I trust myself to possess. Now it's a tallying not of what I have done but what I have left. And the sum I arrive at seems to change every day, like the weather over the lake outside my window. Better that than stasis, I tell myself, and sit down and get on with it.

✳
JUDITH ORTIZ COFER

MOTHERS AND DAUGHTERS

Mourning: a cruel country where I'm no longer afraid.

ROLAND BARTHES

The events in our lives happen in a sequence in time,
but in their significance to ourselves they find their own
order: . . . the continuous thread of revelation.

EUDORA WELTY

"A woman writing thinks back through her mothers," wrote
Virginia Woolf. I have used that quote as an epigraph to various pieces I have written about my grandmother and my
mother, and I have mentally added my own words to it: "and
forward through her daughters."

I have been writing and thinking back through my mother
all of my adult life. As much as my father sacrificed his own
dreams for us, I have never been able to imagine myself as him
nor fully empathize with him. This is unfair, and perhaps it is
as simple as gender, but I think that the truth lies in my fear of

becoming like him. I have always known that I have a propensity for depression, that pessimism is my natural mode. I have a public persona that belies my true nature; within the limited realm of my professional life in academia, and my public life as a writer, I pass for a vivacious Latina. The darkness is known only to those closest to me, and I am fortunate that my family understands and sustains me. I am lucky they are not as afraid of my dark side as I was of my father's. After I emerged from the years of adolescence when I wanted to be nothing like either my mother or father, and particularly after the birth of my daughter, which was also when I began to write poetry, I started to see and envy my mother's resilience, her ability to inhabit the moment.

She and I have talked about her years as the middle daughter in a family of eight; how she loved volleyball and hated becoming a *quinceañera*, which in those days meant announcing to the world a girl's status as a potential wife—nothing like the social extravaganzas of today's young Latinas, but a serious passage into adulthood. My mother said that when she turned fifteen, she began her training in domestic functions such as childcare and cooking that didn't interest her, and she was not allowed to play ball again. In an early poem, I try to capture the mystery of my mother as the reluctant *quinceañera*.

My dolls have been put away like dead
children in a chest I will carry
with me when I marry . . .
My hair/ has been nailed back with my mother's
black hairpins to my skull. Her hands
stretched my eyes open as she twisted
braids into a circle at the nape of my neck . . .

I am wound like the guts of a clock
waiting for each hour to release me.

As a graduate student in an English program and a nascent
writer in the 1970s I found no models in my course readings. I
took what I could where I could find it. Virginia Woolf was the
only woman on my required reading list, and I read her with
a hunger I have rarely experienced; it was not merely knowledge I sought, but an approach, a passageway, to my art. Tell
me what to do, Ms. Woolf. I cannot have a room of my own or
private income (yet); I do not belong to a literary circle, but I
yearn to tell stories, to be a maker with words. And one day,
I discovered a book by Woolf that was not on the syllabus,
a memoir. In its pages, her tone descended slightly from the
Olympian heights of her intellectual style down to a voice in-
flected to an almost sweet yearning for the scraps of memory
that tied her to her childhood—a smell, the breeze stirring
the drapes in her nursery—as she recalled the mother she'd
lost early in her life. I heard in her words the wake-up call I
needed; I understood what she meant when she said that she
had followed the footprints left by strong emotion back to her
"moments of being." I felt that she was speaking to me directly.
I knew I had to let my mother help me locate the footprints
and lead me to the source of my art, *my* moments of being,
and she did.

In her elegy for her husband, *The Year of Magical Thinking*, Joan Didion writes, "Survivors look back and see omens,
messages they missed. . . . They live by symbols" (152). In my
mother's house, I now see signs everywhere that she has been
preparing to leave. She has arranged her bookshelves so that
all the mementoes of my brother's and my lives are organized,

almost as if she expects us to be picking them up soon. She has our report cards, yearbooks, and a scrapbook for each of us containing newspaper clippings, reviews of my books and of the plays my brother acted in, of every little accomplishment or event worthy of being recorded in print. Every notice or clipping I have sent her over the years is taped to a page and dated. She has separate albums for pictures of my family and my brother's. She has my books on one shelf, all signed to "Mi querida madre," several of them dedicated to her and to my daughter Tanya.

"A woman writing thinks back through her mothers." And forward through her daughters. Between my tiny mother and my tall daughter there is a vast distance; yet the daughter with a PhD in mathematics and the grandmother with a minimal education were still so tightly bonded that even the last time we talked, when she told me to be calm and strong for Tanya, my mother called her "mi nena," my baby girl. And Tanya showed her affection even in areas where the vast chasm of world-views between them seemed cosmic. I remember a conversation when Tanya was a student in physics and mathematics, and my mother was telling her about my father, whom she said had come to her after his death. This topic, deeply felt by my mother, that the dead are nearby and accessible, always caused rifts between her and me. I feared that Tanya would eventually be driven away by my mother's superstitious beliefs. Instead, I heard my daughter say gently, "I wish I had known him," and soon they were laughing together over memories of Tanya's control over my father as a toddler. He became totally malleable in her little hands.

But by the time she was two and a half, he was gone. I have discovered that Tanya is much more tolerant of the strangeness of superstition because it is eerily familiar to her as a scientist in an area of mathematics, a field so abstract that it comes to resemble the supernatural realm—at least to the mathematically challenged like me; even in hard science there is a theory of time travel. And in theory, the past and the future exist, working in the same way as the present. I heard a physicist say that the future is already here, and we are merely stepping forward in time to meet it. Ghosts and wormholes. I get to witness my mother and my daughter meeting in a special dimension, beyond time and space. I live in the wormhole between them. I do not believe in ghosts, and I do not understand quantum mechanics, but they represent the *was* and *will be* of my timeline.

Survivors look back and see omens. Everything in my mother's house, in which I wander as if it is the living museum of her, seems ominous and deeply symbolic to me late at night as I begin to say *adios* to her. I see the note by her telephone, the number of a funeral-costs insurance company, and I hang on to it as if it is an important clue left for me to find. When I ask her husband Angel about it, he says that it is something she had been paying into for many years, and she was in the habit of making notes about everything she needed to do. This is something I do too. My students and family laugh at the number of sticky notes I have all over my office, on the covers of books, the dashboard of my car, my dresser mirror. But, I am living by omens and symbols by now, so these little scraps of paper begin to take on immense weight. Why are her shoes lined up in front of her closet, and why is everything folded

so neatly on her shelves? She has never been a domestic goddess and neither am I. She insists on cleanliness but is not a
slave to neatness. Angel says that in the last months she had
wanted a big purging of closets and storage. But this was not
unusual. Over the years I had gotten into the habit of sending her at least one package of clothes, shoes, and other gifts,
almost monthly, and more for her birthday and Christmas. I
knew she loved dressing well, and it was my pleasure to buy
things I thought "looked" like her. I wanted her to have clothes
and shoes people would notice. I knew she liked to say "mi hija
sent them to me." And her house is small, so every year she
had a great giveaway to other female relatives and her church.
I liked knowing that she could now do this, be generous with
others, for during our Paterson and Augusta days clothing
money usually was spent frugally on my brother and me.

We didn't live in poverty; we lived cautiously on the outer
edge of lower-middle-class status. As military dependents, we
had the basics and no more, but we never went hungry. We
had doctors when we needed them, and we could pay our rent,
even if not always on time. But extras were a rare privilege. For
instance, my mother and I could not both buy new dresses on
the same shopping trip, and while I never thought this meant
we were poor, I know it's why I have indulged her in clothes
over the years. As I take inventory of my mother's life, it is not
the material part of this that gives me solace, but rather that
each item represents a smile, a moment of pleasure, and that
I contributed to her sense of herself as beautiful, and worthy,
and of being well loved by me. Her closet is like one of those
department store racks she so loved to go through, replete
with outfits in the tropical colors that looked best on her *café*

con leche skin. I count thirty-seven pairs of size-five shoes, all in a neat row, all ready to transport her, *aqui y alla*, anywhere she wished to go.

I am looking for a way to connect *the continuous thread of revelation* of her life in every word I read, every object I see or remember, and every photograph that has even the most minimal remnant of a memory of my mother. I am trying to inhabit my grief fully so that when she is gone, I will eventually think of her without an overwhelming sense of loss. I know I am still aboard a two-propeller six-passenger *avioneta* on my way to the cruel country that Barthes claims is the state of mourning. I know I haven't even arrived yet. My mother's presence feels insistent in all her things in her house, yet across town she is slipping away. I must find a way to comprehend that fact. I must learn how to manage my pain and make good on what she has left me—not these things, but that insistent energy.

One of the old photos I have on my iPad, taken during one of our frequent returns to my grandmother's house in Puerto Rico while my father was on one of his extended tours of duty with the navy, is of a group of my Island playmates posing in the middle of what looks like a park, with a hill rising above us and distant palm trees. Standing close together in a sort of cluster are eight children between five and eight years of age, including my mother's youngest siblings—an aunt, who is only two years older than I am, and my uncle, one year older— my brother, and three neighbor girls, one of whom was my closest friend. I'll call her M. When one of M's sisters visits my mother in the hospital I show her the picture. She smiles, and then she points to her older sister, my best friend in those days.

"You know she died of breast cancer." I have a vague memory of this, but the words "cancer" and "death" did not resonate with me then as they do now. I shut down my electronic photo album. I do not want to talk about death in front of my mother. Later I will ask M for the whole story; later I am hungry for stories of inexplicable illness, needy for the parallel narratives that will comfort me in my misery. I will then open myself up to the company and the tales of fellow sufferers, so that I can stop myself from asking, "Why her, Why now, Why me?" I will nod my head and pretend I understand the constant reliance on blind faith. I will hear again and again about a God who takes and takes: *God took my sister at fifty-two, my daughter at twenty-three, my son when he was a teenager. . . .* It is always *his will, his right.* I will have to swallow this placebo, and hope it will work on me as it obviously has on so many.

Eudora Welty found that in writing, as well as in life, "The excursion is the same when you go looking for your sorrow as when you go looking for your joy." As I look at this picture of us in that field, a series of associations come to me that may seem paradoxical, but are really an alchemical compound made up equally of lead and gold. The "field" where we played was really a fenced-off pasture that belonged to the American sugar processing company. At the top of the hill stood a large white house where the American company manager and his family lived behind a grove of palm trees. *La casa grande* was fenced in and screened in. Many towns had a big house where an American family lived, and at that time only these houses had mosquito screens. We hung mosquito nets over our beds, but lived with windows and doors thrown wide open, as if in

the belief that mosquitoes waited until nightfall to strike na-
tives. I never questioned it, but as children from "afuera," my
brother and I learned to live with a layer of calamine lotion
over the exposed parts of our bodies, because mosquitoes,
our playmates told us, mocking our fake-pink faces and arms,
liked the fresh meat of gringos best and could identify us by
our foreign smell.

The pasture was accessible from my grandmother's house
through a thick area of plants, trees, and vines, where guavas
and banana plants grew wild. Making our way through the
vegetation, we often stepped on a magical kind of grass called
morivivi that folded into itself when you touched it, then came
back after a while. It resurrected. At the top of the hill was a
gigantic mango tree with limbs as thick as most trees' trunks.
It had huge knots at its base where the women sat to embroi-
der, have coffee from a thermos, and watch us play.

We called the tree *el barco*, the ship, and we managed to
lower a huge limb down over the hill so some of us could sit on
it while other made it sway—a feeling that, to this day, I find
beyond compare. It was not a carnival ride; it had not been
constructed by adults. It was the pure product of childhood
imagination and effort. We were allowed to tumble and roll
down the grassy hill, and to gather wild guavas and ripe ba-
nanas from the unfenced section, but we were forbidden to go
near the American's house, especially since a huge white horse
had occasionally been spotted grazing nearby. But I could see
fruit trees growing near the house, and I just knew whatever
was growing there would be like nothing I had tasted before.
So one day, when all the children had been sent to the bed-
rooms to take an afternoon siesta, I snuck out still wearing
only my underwear (my mother ensured that we would not

get out of the house by insisting that we take off our clothes before a nap), and I ran through the woods, past our ship, and up the hillside. All I remember after that is the sight of that horse galloping toward me and my dash to the nearest exit out of the pasture, which happened to be a barbed-wire fence, which I dove through. The gash in the lumbar region of my back sent my mother into hysteria. I was rushed to the nearest neighbor who had a car and to the hospital, where I got a tetanus shot. The next day I got a premium spanking from my mother, and I was ordered to sit down at the table and write a letter to my father. My mother wanted me to tell him exactly what had happened. She always feared his anger when something bad happened to us, as he constantly reminded her that her main obligation while she was at her mothers' house was our health and safety. I don't remember my exact words to him.

But this was my first written story, and I must have made it a contrite one, because a couple of weeks later I received a pair of dolls from Athens, Greece, where his ship was currently anchored, both wearing skirts, so my entire family sat around puzzling out whether they were both females. They arrived in the same package from which my mother received her painted shell from Capri; the same one in which, fifty years in the future, I would find cigarette ashes.

Near that painted shell on her dresser are several framed pictures of my brother and me as awkward teenagers. One is a picture of me I have always hated. I look like an impostor. I am wearing a zebra-striped shirtdress and ugly pointy shoes, and I'm sporting my new Twiggy haircut. It was taken on the day we boarded the Pan Am airbus for my first trip back as a teenager to Puerto Rico, and on that day I hated my parents. I hated my mother most of all for putting her nostalgic need for her *casa* and *familia* ahead of *my* need for a normal life. It will be a bad interlude for us. I will be in full rebellion. I've dressed as outrageously as possible, especially for the flight there, so I can make an entrance at my grandmother's. Once there, I will refuse to follow my mother's rules, refuse to visit relatives with her, refuse to attend Sunday mass. During an argument over an unchaperoned trip to the beach with friends I desperately want to go on, I will tell her that she is everything I do not want to grow up to be. I will tell her in front of her mother and sisters that she is a relic and an embarrassment to me; I'll tell her I hate the Island and the crowded house we live in with her many loud relatives. I'll swear to her that when I'm on my own I will never return.

I remember her tears, her escape into her mother's bedroom, and the hushed women's voices. I knew they were advising her about dealing with me. I remember them trying hard to make peace between my mother and me. I disdained them, ignoring their attempts to talk to me by hiding my face behind a book. I wanted nothing more than to get back to *my* world. I had friends in Paterson where I was beginning to find my way out of the barrio. All I wanted to do was get back to my almost-American life.

For the next couple of years, I plugged myself in to my transistor radio and stopped talking about anything of consequence with my parents. In a poem I later tried to use the photograph to reconnect with the fifteen-year-old who, like my mother as a *quinceañera*, was *wound like the guts of a clock, waiting for each hour to release her*, although it is only now, at the moment I write these words, that I connect my mother to me at around the same age.

Writing transforms. And, on the page, it is always *now*. In "Here Is a Picture of Me" I write, "I am skinny and brash, thirteen or fourteen / aware of my bones, of the angles and curves / reforming my skin . . . / My parents are outside the frame, waiting / to see if the present moment can really / be captured on film."

I claim no expertise on photography, but I can feel its strong kinship to writing: capturing a moment on the page through the carefully chosen image. Images in a frame, on paper, in the brain, at the moment of death. We live and die with a slide show in our minds.

The events in our lives happen in a sequence in time, but time itself is a human construct, an invented artifice, a scaffold to sustain the illusion of order in the chaos. Childhood years, teenage years, early adulthood, and so on, seem to fall neatly into a timeline, but as I watch my mother come to the end of her days, memories come to me more like photos in my randomly ordered electronic album. There are pictures of my grandson Eli at birth interspersed with pictures of Tanya as a baby, then a young bride, then more of Eli, dozens of Eli, and then the old photos of my brother and me on tricycles in front of our first suburban house. . . . I fight an impulse to show them to her now, to try to get her to open her eyes, which by now show only a gray milkiness on the rare occasions when she flutters them halfway open.

What is it that evades analysis in a photo, that makes one respond as if to an image lingering from a dream? Barthes looked for the ineffable something that made his mother her own unique and irreproducible self, and he found it finally in a photo of her at five years of age. That ineffable something was, of course, beyond words—a way of remembering her that would mean nothing to you or me. In fact, the photo does not appear in the book. Barthes writes, "It exists only for me. For you, it would be nothing but an indifferent picture." I look and keep looking at these photos, out of sequence, out of any order in time, but representing my past, present, and future. I wonder whether her slideshow has begun, the one all those near-death-experience witnesses claim happens as a sort of prelude to the tunnel of light. Which photos have you chosen, Mami? Please, not the one of me in that hideous zebra-striped dress, Puerto Rican Twiggy with an attitude, ready to use words to hurt you.

The next morning—the day before she will die—I see a huge yellow caterpillar making its slow, meandering way from the front yard by way of the carport. It seems to be heading drunkenly toward me. Before I leave for the hospital, I note its progress—only a third of the way to the grass in her garden. I imagine the world from his perspective: a hard surface, vast distance, threatening dark shadow (me) lurking above. Danger. Danger. I make sure not to step on him as I rush out. That night, when I sit on my mother's rocker to sort through my fears from the day before I try to sleep, I look around for the caterpillar. I finally locate him at the bottom of the hibiscus bush.

I hope it will be a good enough refuge for him.

TOI DERRICOTTE

After twenty years at my university, I'm retiring. I taught my last classes last week and on Sunday had a dinner party for my graduate students, doing far too much work in order to make it perfect. Since it's the Christmas holidays, I decorated with "notations" of the season: outside, seven large red and gold balls hanging on the baby crab apple tree; inside, a mantel with several kinds and colors of evergreen branches with a few battery-operated candles (I swear they twinkle softly just like the real thing); a huge white poinsettia in the window upstairs. The house smells faintly of wet fresh pine.

I cooked for two days, making my mom's New Orleans Italian spaghetti sauce, rich, dark, and thick with meat, with the strangest necessary ingredient: two cans of those soggy-looking mushrooms that, for some reason stay, for two and a half hours of simmering, whole buttons like belly buttons, and give up a woody essence that fresh mushrooms do not. Italian bread drenched with garlic, butter, parsley, and parmesan, oven-baked until crisp across the top.

The students were appreciative, bringing salad and desserts—the most beautiful apple pie with a crust that looked like thick ruffles—and staying until I was very tired and very ready to say goodnight. I had surprised myself at the dinner table, feeling a tinge of sadness that, try as I might, I couldn't shake.

So much has changed so quickly in the past year. And I can't be sure how accurate my memory is, so even as I report it I wonder if I'm remembering right. Now, for example, I'm in constant pain from arthritis in my knees, feet, and hands. And that is definitely either new, or new to conscious admission. It's true that I have been able not to notice pain. All my life I have been able to walk around with a bruise the size of a hand and have no idea how it happened or where it came from. It's as if, at the same time I hurt myself, a little piece of steel slides in to push the memory down and hide it. I suppose it's a habit from childhood. My father couldn't stand crying or complaining—"I'll give you something to cry about"—especially if it was he who had caused the pain. I held my body in duck-and-dodge mode, psychologically too. And while it definitely saved me a great deal of hardship and pain—perhaps even saved my life! (because my father was, I believe, capable of murder)— it caused me to take some very unnatural poses; so now, like those football players who took the hard knocks, it's starting to show that things aren't stacked up right: my balance was and is unsteady, shifty. And that isn't good for the knees.

But the worst change is in my memory, how I need to make a hundred trips a day up and down the stairs because I can only hold one thing in my mind at a time. Lists are endless, everywhere, but as much as I try to sort things out and make them manageable, the lists themselves, with their mashed-up and provoking demands, are a constant source of anxiety and dread.

After fifteen years, it seemed to me that I was ready to be on my own. After therapy for most of my life (and therapists who were my first safe family, who truly were devoted to me, who listened, cared, and even, I believe, suffered with me through years of my unending struggles with fear and self-loathing), I said, "I don't feel I need to be seen anymore." And I meant much more than the "seeing" that is done when you go in for a doctor's appointment: I meant that seeing by an almighty eye that is patient, kind, and loving. The eye that had weekly rained down on me the knowledge that I was of value had suddenly moved out of the sky of that office into the office of my heart. Now I am able to see myself.

Did I use up the last drop of suffering when I finished my last book? It was the book that I had been studying to write all my life, the story of the violence in my childhood. It took that long to give what was unendurable "a local habitation and a name," to make it an object separate from me. I think of what Carolyn Kizer said, how we always see the faults of our parents when we're young but, as we get older, we begin to see who we are, and the effect we have had on others. God knows I never was one easy to live with. I am, must be—the way I suffer at night in bed to make the cover exactly even over my ears, the top of my head, that place on my back where my top sometimes hikes up and exposes some skin on my back—the most sensitive creature on the planet. The length of time it takes to get things exactly right, my legs in exactly the right position is, must be, entirely different from normal. My body is excruciat-ingly exact in its demands.

Once a psychologist gave me a test in which I had to notice what was out of place in fifty drawings. I sped through them, finding every little dot in an instant. When he shut the book he said, either you're a genius or crazy. It's true, violence in your childhood, fearing every second for your life, can make you focus. But maybe it's as my mother always said, it wasn't as bad as I made it out to be.

So what will I write about now that the old sources are used up? When I am so-called free?

So often during the past fifty years, when I had to support myself, I thought of Rilke and the ten years the countess sup-ported him as he lived, ate, slept, walked about in fear (in the castle) that he'd never write again, staying solitary, refusing even to go to his only daughter's wedding, waiting in dread and de-termination for what had to happen, that he would write the *Duino Elegies*.

I thought of what it would have been like if some patron, some husband, some partner, some lover of art, some teacher had said to me: *you are a great writer, Toi, let me support you until you write your next book.* I always had to work, I had to get out of school quickly because I had a child when I was twenty and I had to support him, I began substitute teach-ing even before I graduated. We were living in the projects. I have been teaching since I was twenty, even before that if you count teaching Sunday school and keeping kids in order at church. I have been teaching for over fifty years, and now I believe I've got enough in my retirement account—even though half of those years I was paid by the hour and had no benefits or plans—now, I have saved hard and saved enough to be my own patron, to be the countess who is confident that, no matter how much time it takes, I will produce something of enough value. It's good it's taken this long. I think on some level I planned it this way. I don't think, even if I had had a countess, that it was time, that I myself believed enough to have done my part.

Even when I did receive grants, I'm not so sure I wrote any more than I did when I was teaching, as if there is a normal flow, a spleen, a regulating function no matter how much time you have. And yet I cling to my reason that now, retired, I will write more, and not just because I have more time, but because I believe that I am a writer; when I sit down to the paper, I am able to say this exorbitant thing to myself: today (and not after another twenty years of therapy and revision), I am going to create something of value.

And so I am writing this essay today, this essay on aging, on being a woman and writing.

And I realize that writing is never my subject, that really all my subjects are metaphors for what I am truly writing about, that writing itself is a metaphor for my subject, which is always the body.

How do I know who I am except by how it feels to be inside this truck of a body?

Yesterday I was describing to a few friends how I felt when I received several writers' awards this year. This is not to say these awards weren't validating, that they didn't give me confidence and a sense of my worth as a human being, but, at the same time, I must admit there was a sense of harshness in the moment when I walked up to the stage, that intense spotlight rained on me, and, in my mind, it was not a kind eye. I wrestled with my footing, as they say, skating on thin ice. Was the thin ice that feeling of temporality, the falseness or at least the fleetingness of a hunk of glass or metal to hold on to? Perhaps it was the memory of that fleet moment when you hold the finished poem in your hands? These could be the reasons why I stood at the podium in a defining dress and pearls, an accomplished person graciously smiling and conveying my gratitude and, all the while, paddling, paddling.

This year I made over twenty thousand dollars in awards. Money which goes into that retirement fund, for it suddenly hit me hard that retirement doesn't only mean that I will not be teaching, it means that I won't be getting a paycheck.

All right. What if I were to make more money writing than I did teaching? I know that's crazy to think. But perhaps this new writing I'm doing won't need to drag my readers through hell in order to pay off. Perhaps my truth is a bit easier to swallow now that I'm not dragging around the corpses of my childhood. Now it's just me in here. I feel my truths are in a way less personal, less threatening, I feel allied with any other woman, any other person heading in the direction to which we all must eventually turn.

*

GAIL GODWIN

WORKING ON THE ENDING

When you're a young writer, you subtract the birth dates of authors from their publication dates and feel panic or hope. When you're an old writer, you observe the death dates of your favorite writers and you reflect on their works and their lives.

Two years ago I outlived Henry James, who died two months short of his seventy-third birthday. In his final years, he wrote an autobiography of his childhood, befriended badly wounded World War I soldiers, and changed his citizenship. I have catapulted myself out of many writing setbacks and humiliations with the rallying cry of the dying novelist Dencombe, in James's story "The Middle Years": "We work in the dark—we do what we can—we give what we have. Our doubt is our passion, and our passion is our task." The words have the stride of a march and the echo of a mantra. Already I have missed being able to ask James, "When you were my age, what did you do when . . . ?"

"How does what you want out of writing change with age?" Terry Gross asked Philip Roth on NPR's *Fresh Air* in October

2010. Roth, seventy-seven, told her it hadn't changed much for him. He wanted to be as alert and energetic as ever at the keyboard, he wanted to be taken seriously, and he wanted to make a work of art out of his subject.

You want to be taken seriously; that doesn't change. What has changed for me is the degree of compromise I am willing to inflict on my work in order to see it in print. As a young writer, I was told by the fiction editor at *Esquire* that he'd publish my story if I took out the woman's dreams. I took them out. "It will make her more inscrutable," he promised, chuckling. It certainly did. Forty years later, "A Sorrowful Woman" is my most anthologized story, and I get regular e-mails from bewildered high school and college students asking why this woman did what she did.

Now, after having worked with all varieties of editors, I like to think I have built a pretty impervious fortress against wrongheaded suggestions. ("Would you consider having Francis and Alice marry at the end of *The Good Husband*?") But only last year my fortress cracked under pressure from marketing forces. ("If you call this novel *The Red Nun*, you will lose thousands of readers. Too many people have a bad nun in their past.") I caved and went with the last two words of what was to have been the novel's subtitle: *A Tale of Unfinished Desires*. Would I make that choice again? No. But I will continue to urge professionals to tell me what I have failed to make clear and what needs development. ("Does Mother Ravenel have a secret?" an editor asked me after his first reading of *Unfinished Desires*. I had mistakenly assumed everyone guessed what her secret was. His question stimulated me to add a scene—and an important dream.)

When I was a young writer, I would jump-start the next

project as soon as I completed the last. "You have been too damn lazy," I scolded myself after having lost faith in a story started the day after sending off the final draft of my first novel to its publisher. Back then I believed it was more productive and honorable to hop into the saddle and strike off for somewhere rather than just lie around.

Now I do a lot of lying around. Finally I have accepted that my supine dithering is fertile and far from a waste of time. As a young writer I heard the old Borges tell his rapt audience at the Iowa Writers' Workshop that blindness had taught him to write his stories in his head. Ah, to be able to do that, I remember thinking, if only you didn't have to go blind. I still have my eyesight, but within the past year I have discovered I can compose whole paragraphs in my head and find them waiting, intact, next morning.

Inevitable for the old writer is the slowdown of word retrieval. You pause over the keyboard and summon in vain a word you need. This happens oftener and oftener, until you find your jotting pad crammed with thesaurus numbers (74.17, 658.11, 215.22, 236.2). All it once took was the slightest tug at the bell for the vigorous servant, accompanied by backup synonyms, to report for duty. Now you wait, and this waiting offers a variety of responses. You can rail at your "senior moment" like those tiresome people who bring a conversation to a halt because they can't remember the name of a place or person. You can, of course, resort to your ragged thesaurus, unless your moment is so dire you can't even remember any words for the concept you're trying to describe. You can *do without* the word and perhaps realize how little you needed it, especially if it happened to be an adjective or an adverb. Or you can leave a blank, to be filled in later. You can also take a break from your work and read some poetry (which is all about compression and word selection), or dip into Samuel Beckett's late novel *Worstward Ho*, an old writer's celebration of reduced options. ("Fail again, fail better.") If you are not thrilled by how much his stripped language (he called it "unwording the world") can do, you will come away with a revised perspective on how many words a writer can do without.

For me, a consolation prize of word delay has been an increased intolerance for the threadbare phrase. I don't want anyone on my pages to "burst into tears" or "just perceptibly" do anything, ever again. Better to take a break and ask: "What exactly do I want to say here? How does this really look?" I'll ask myself, "How do you describe the way an old couple walk that shows they have been *walking together for decades*?" That in itself may turn out to be the best description.

The old writer hopes to do credit to the material that has been hers or his alone. *"I was there / Me in place and the place in me,"* Seamus Heaney testifies in "A Herbal." You become more urgent about your vital themes (what I really care about is whether this girl will develop or abandon her moral center) and less patient with peripheries (how much more war research do I need for this minor character, anyway?).

Another seasoned writer, the eighty-two-year-old Cynthia Ozick, pays homage in her novel, *Foreign Bodies*, to her lifelong idol Henry James by marrying her quite different strengths to his in *The Ambassadors*.

In his seventy-ninth year, Carl Jung wrote to his friend the Reverend Victor White that a complete life consisted of accepting without reservation "the particular fatal tissue in which one finds oneself embedded," and trying to "make sense of it or to create a cosmos from the chaotic mess into which one is born."

The old writer wants to use up his fatal tissue like biscuit dough, pushing the leftovers into another and another artful shape—down to the last strange little animal. Eva Trout, the eponymous heroine of Elizabeth Bowen's final novel, published the year she turned sixty-nine, is a triumph of Bowen animal dough. Eva is the larger-than-life, some would say monstrous, culmination of a subject that haunted Bowen's work: the neglected, or misplaced, child. The eighty-one-year-old Saul Bellow's slim novella *The Actual,* published three years before the heftier *Ravelstein*, distills his abiding attraction to "first-class noticers" into a Chicago romance with fairy-tale elements, in which a lifelong noticer is sought out and rewarded for his gift.

I will be very interested to meet my strange little animals.

*

PATRICIA HENLEY

THE POTHOLDER MODEL OF LITERARY AMBITION

Writing short stories reminds me of my eight-year-old self, in the 1950s, making cotton potholders on a little steel loom and selling them door to door for twenty-five cents each. At night I'd sit in bed and weave those loops and crochet the edges, all the while practicing my spiel, and dreaming of what I'd buy with the quarters. Wax lips and bubble gum. *Archie* comic books. Nail polish—although my father forbade nail polish. I lived in Terre Haute, Indiana, in a neighborhood of muddy playgrounds and ma-and-pa groceries. It had a fallen-down feel, as if the houses were the architectural equivalent of a girl who wouldn't stand up straight and proud. I couldn't wait to get out of there, to places with more shine. I wanted to be a writer.

I try to place myself in that girl's mind to recall what that meant exactly. It would be a life of reading, of slight domestic disorder, books and papers stacked beside a desk, libraries, visits to cities, unpredictability, eccentric people, cataloguing all the rich details of life lived outdoors, for I experienced an intense euphoria outdoors as a child—reinforced by reading *The Secret Garden* over and over. It would be a life of travel, although the farthest I traveled as a child was Columbus, Ohio. My travel experiences came from books—*Marjorie Morningstar* and *Jane Eyre* and *A Tree Grows in Brooklyn*. I think of Joan Didion in her essay about becoming a writer. She said that she wasn't a very good student at Berkeley because she was always more interested in the way sunlight moved across her hardwood floor than in her classes. A sensualist. And I felt that in myself.

From reading writers' biographies, I understood that ambition might be a bright thread in the fabric of a life or it might be the entire cloth. Within ambition were the seeds of profound disappointment and delirious acceptance. Jo March of *Little Women* was like a big sister to me. "She did not think herself a genius by any means, but when the writing fit came on, she gave herself up to it with entire abandon, and led a blissful life, unconscious of want, care, or bad weather, while she sat safe and happy in an imaginary world. . . . The divine afflatus usually lasted a week or two, and then she emerged from her 'vortex,' hungry, sleepy, cross, or despondent." I have known the bliss of the vortex. Blissful more was the realization of ambition, the moment when Jo March received the check for a hundred dollars; she had won the literary prize. She was delighted with the encouragement in the letter, *and* she loved being able to send her mother and sister to the seashore with the money.

This time of longing in your life is beautiful. All possibilities are ahead of you. You think you want to make something happen, but when it does—you finally publish a story, you publish a book, someone reviews your book favorably—you realize that the bliss lies in the moment you pluck a metaphor from thin air. It lies in the time spent at your desk.

I began my adult writing life as a poet. My reasonable ambition was to see one or two poems published in magazines around Baltimore, where I lived, mostly, from 1970 until 1974. In 1979, when I became ill and was required to spend almost two months in bed or lounging around, I turned to fiction to save my sanity. I wrote the beginning of a novel, but that petered out because I had no sense of structure. I had no teacher. I finally settled on short stories and wrote the stories in *Friday Night at Silver Star* from 1979 through 1984. I wrote another novel that went in the drawer. And then another. But they weren't tied to ambition; I wrote them because I delighted in the sensual world I was creating.

The publication of *Friday Night at Silver Star* allowed me to apply for a teaching job that would give me more time to write. I was hired for a visiting position at Purdue University, and I have been there for twenty-one years. At first I went on writing stories and looked to the careers of Alice Munro and Andre Dubus and Raymond Carver as writers worth emulating, writers who wrote stories rather than novels.

But in 1989 I started the novel that would become *Hummingbird House*. Many interruptions later, many drafts discarded, I finished it in the summer of 1996 while on sabbatical in New Mexico. I was charmed by every aspect of the sabbatical experience: long hours at the dining room table, a view of the Sangre de Cristo Mountains out my window, and then, in the afternoon, hikes at Georgia O'Keeffe's Ghost Ranch, and then dinner with my husband, a little wine, a little fire in our adobe house, occasional trips to Santa Fe for a movie, always in the vortex of writing and dreaming about writing, with no teaching to disturb the flow. It was like running a marathon, hard, but sweet in its simplicity. I wanted more of that. Craved it. My life was suddenly infused with literary ambition—ambition laced with an irony bred of my subject matter, the lives of women and children in wartime.

I felt called on a near spiritual level to write *Hummingbird House* and knew that I would do it no matter what the outcome. But I'll be frank: I wanted solid reviews, freedom from teaching, cold cash in the bank, and a relationship with a publishing house with resources. It took two difficult years to find a publisher for the book, years in which I felt like a fraud while teaching. I'd spent seven years writing a novel that no one wanted to publish. Then surprisingly good things began to happen, in quick succession: Fred Ramey at MacMurray & Beck in Denver accepted the manuscript and did a superb edit on it in record time; it was a finalist for the 1999 National Book Award and the *New Yorker* Fiction Prize; it was nominated by the Chicago Public Library for the IMPAC Dublin Award. I never knew who might be calling when the phone rang. People would ask me, "What's it like, being a finalist for the National Book Award?" And I'd usually say, "The first thing I thought was 'What am I going to wear?'" It had nothing to do with writing, but it was a good time, those few months.

My audience had expanded; of course, I wanted to write another novel. *In the River Sweet* came much faster. By that time I had a wonderful agent who sold the book based on the first thirty-nine pages of manuscript. More than one publisher wanted to buy it: the stuff of writerly daydreams. Finally. I bought a house in the country, with horses as my nearest neighbors, perfect for writing. I went to Vietnam to research *In the River Sweet.* I was fifty-three years old. I had more confidence in whatever ideas took hold in me, and I had plenty of ideas.

When *In the River Sweet* came out, I traveled for five weeks to nineteen cities, from Seattle to Boston. Some of the appearances were at colleges and universities, but at least half were book tour events arranged by my publisher. They put me up in the most luxurious hotels, like the Monaco in Chicago, where you may ask to have a goldfish in a bowl brought to your room if you miss your pets.

But the tour went awry. Most writers whose books had been scheduled for publication in September 2002 were shoved into October because of the first 9/11 commemoration, which meant we were competing for air time and bookstore time. Barnes and Noble had not "gotten behind the book." Borders had named it an Original Voices pick for October 2002, but I was not booked into a single Borders. *The Lovely Bones* had come out in paperback, and I would go into a bookstore to find one or two copies of *In the River Sweet* and waist-high stacks of *The Lovely Bones*. I had heard writers complain about how disappointing book tours are, but I had been naïve and thought that surely my publishers, having spent so much money for the book, would see to it that it sold. They didn't. I found out that you can write a good book, be published by a New York house, be sent on an expensive tour, and still feel like a ghost in those hotels and bookstores.

John Gardner wrote that writing a novel is a "sustained psychological battle with yourself." Still, I had energy for that battle. I laid out my plans for another novel. Perhaps my inability to find a title that my editor liked should have been a warning sign. I wanted *Tango Season;* she felt that sounded like a mystery novel. In February 2003 I went to New York City to scope out the possibility of doing the down-in-the-street research, setting a novel there and in Bucks County, Pennsylvania, a country-mouse-versus-city-mouse sort of story. I might be an outsider, I thought, but I'll just move wherever I want, write about whatever I choose. I had spent five months in Central America, researching *Hummingbird House.* I had traveled to Vietnam and spent time in New Orleans to get what I needed to write *In the River Sweet.* I love unearthing history, interviewing people, and keeping a notebook of the felt life of a place I'm visiting.

But at the end of that long reconnaissance trip in New York, my editor sat me down in a coffee shop in Greenwich Village and told me, "Don't set this book in New York." I was baffled, stunned. She sees me as the country mouse, I thought—a writer from the hinterlands who can't get New York right. I went home to the Midwest, changed the setting of the book to Chicago, wrote draft after draft that the editor rejected, and, finally, two years later, broke off my relationship with that publishing house. I am still paying back the advance, so every month when I write the check I am reminded of my failure. The manuscript—*Home Plate*—was rejected by other publishing houses, until it came clear that this was another novel for the drawer.

I had given that editor enormous power over my writing life, and her criticism eroded my self-confidence. Now, when I have an ambitious idea for a novel, instead of thinking, "That would be a great thing to explore for a few years," I can't help but think, "What if it doesn't work out?" And I do not have a relationship with a publisher I can count on, only wisps of connection to the two publishers who keep my books in print. Perhaps to withstand such disappointments, you need to have an equal measure of longing. And that sort of longing is mostly for the young.

But I have built into my body and mind, at a cellular level, the practice of writing. I wake up between five and six every morning with stories and language seducing me. I get up, have a cup of strong coffee, and in my red flannel L.L. Bean robe go to my computer. A few years ago it seemed natural to start writing short stories again. Stories slot nicely into the seasonal demands of being a teacher. It's easy to abandon a piece or set a first draft aside and start another. You can cannibalize the novels in your drawer for material. When you do finish, you have the satisfaction of completing a small, neatly made object.

A short story is a humble piece of work, to be peddled to the little magazines, almost like selling potholders to your neighbors. I do not mind this life, with its focus on the small object, given to a small audience of serious readers, who might years from now meet me at a reading and say, "I remember that story." I still remember where I was—Stanley Park in Vancouver on a dampish day—when, with a sense of wonder, I read Alice Munro's "Red Dress—1946." Riding out to Old Faithful on Christmas Eve in a snowcat, I read Richard Ford's "Winterkill." Both stories marked me as a writer. They are short pieces that forever changed my life. You might even say they were useful.

Perhaps as a younger writer I was in too big a hurry. Donald Hall recommends working on a poem for ten years before publishing it. William Gass once said to me, "It takes about ten years to learn to write a good sentence." Writers of another generation, I thought, an older generation, believe in this patient approach. And now, I am *of* them, tinkering with my stories for years.

I traded that house in the country for a house in town. Ambition moved on, like a sweetheart you bid good riddance. Now, at the age of sixty-five, as the school bus chugs by on my street, I'm still in my robe at the computer, but I have no more ambition than this on a wintry morning: to take my time making the small, memorable story that moves a reader in one sitting. To practice writing as Isak Dinesen suggested we should. "I write a little every day, without hope, without despair."

✳
ERICA JONG

When I tell people my mother is a hundred and a half, that my grandfather lived to ninety-eight and my father to ninety-three, they look at me approvingly and say "You've got good genes" as if they are about to find a new reason to be envious. They have no idea what they're saying. My mother no longer speaks—she who was once a great talker, reader, painter—no longer recognizes anyone, and sleeps most of the time, peeing in her diapers. If these are good genes, spare me. Living to a century is a crock. I don't see the joy of it. And I am saying it now while I still can.

I never expected to get this old—certainly not old enough to be in an anthology about women writers of a certain age. In some ways we never age. I get as excited about writing a poem as I ever did. The question is whether other people get as excited about poems about aging as they do about poems of first love. The subjects that interest us as we age are often invisible to the young. I get excited about my grandchildren, but there's nothing new about that. And our society is in love with the new. As we age, our writing ages with us and sometimes we wonder if anybody cares but other women of a certain age. Yes, they are the most avid readers, but often they are readers whose taste goes unconsidered and unmarked. The young are the important tastemakers, and if we write about the ironies of aging, perhaps they can't identify.

I certainly couldn't identify when my grandfather complained that he only had *me* to talk to because "all my friends are dead." Only now does his complaint resonate with me. Not all my friends are dead, but many are—and many enemies too. Strangely, I don't exult when they die. Competitors are as necessary as fans. There is an emptiness when they go.

My grandchildren thrill me with their newness, their discovery of the world. Their need to learn new things—swimming, painting, history—delights me. When my granddaughter says to her twin brother that he can't cut off her head because she is *not* Anne Boleyn but Queen Elizabeth the First, I cheer. At four and a half, both twins demand historicity even in play.

Poetry and grandchildren never cease to delight, like music. Other things drop away—rituals like charity benefits, the endless jousting for social position, become boring—as do literary awards, once you have sat on enough committees and realize how arbitrary they are, how much horse-trading goes on, and how nearly always, the compromise candidate rather than the most radical and fresh voice wins.

Youth still beguiles us—but with a new slant. It excites us, and at first we think we want to relive it. But eventually we realize that seeing youth through the eyes of history is a particular vantage point we wouldn't want to lose. That dream of being young again *knowing what you know now* is a delusion.

At times it is a wished-for delusion, but when you really think it through you realize all that would be lost—the irony, the double vision which innocence cannot have. Perhaps that is also why we long for the naïveté of small children. Doubleness of vision is a burden as well as a delight.

I am writing a novel now in which a woman of a certain age longs to travel back through time and be young again. But eventually she comes to understand that she cannot choose which moments in her youth to visit and is forced to relive as much pain as joy. Time-travel is tricky, as most time-travelers discover. At first we think we'll regain our dewy looks, our enthusiasm, our joy in the newness of love and lust, but we are dumbstruck to learn that we might also have to live our pain again, our unformed identities, our confusions.

While it's fun to time-travel in books, to recreate our youthful selves with the hindsight of irony, it's also fun to write about who we are now, as we age in utterly unexpected ways. Our youthful selves seem so unknowing and our present selves too much so. If only we could find an intelligent middle ground between the two!

The search for voice in our books becomes more difficult as we age. When young we only had to learn to write as we spoke—both aloud and in our own heads. As we grow older we strain to find a voice that both age and youth will thrill to—a much harder task.

Youth has a kick, the excitement of the new. Age may sound too world-weary. Think of the writers who thrilled you with their viridity, if not virility—Ernest Hemingway, Kurt Vonnegut, J. D. Salinger—and see how they aged. Hemingway's voice palled unless he was writing out of his youth, as in *A Move-*

able Feast. Vonnegut became grumpy unless he had a real historical event to describe, like the fire-bombing of Dresden in *Slaughterhouse-Five.* And Salinger refused to age at all. Where are his hidden unpublished books?

These are all writers I've loved, but they show how difficult aging is for American writers. And for women writers, as we deepen from the voice of the ingénue to that of the wise woman, it's even worse. Few have mastered this metamorphosis except in memoir. Maybe this is because of our prejudice against old crones—wise or not. And why do we hold on to this prejudice? Out of fear? Intimidation? Ursula Le Guin once wrote in an essay entitled "The Space Crone": "Faced with the fulfilled Crone, all but the bravest men wilt and retreat, crestfallen and cockadroop." Perhaps it is the Crone's breadth and depth of experience we find so frightening. As Le Guin goes on to explain, life has required that she change seamlessly from one phase of womanhood to another, a remarkable feat that gives her a kind of wisdom and knowing that only the Crone can possess:

> She was a virgin once, a long time ago, and then a sexually potent fertile female, and then went through menopause. She has given birth several times and faced death several times—the same times. She is facing the final birth/death a little more nearly and clearly every day now. . . . She has a stock of sense, wit, patience, and experiential shrewdness. . . . She knows, though she won't admit it, that Dr. Kissinger has not gone and will never go where she has gone, that the scientists and shamans have not done what she has done.

Perhaps we neglect to listen to her wisdom for fear of its veracity.

Doris Lessing found a voice for the aging intelligent woman in *The Golden Notebook*—which is probably why so many love it. And Francine du Plessix Gray found a middle-aged voice to chronicle her parents' lives in *Them: A Memoir of Parents*. Colette wrote about female old age, but not in fiction—except for Lea renouncing love in *The Last of Chéri*.

Our great classic English writers like Jane Austen and Charlotte Brontë did not explore the subject—either because they didn't live long enough or thought it uninteresting. Edith Wharton grew old but explored the ironies of age through the tragedy of *Ethan Frome*—her most atypical and, oddly, most taught novel.

It was a male writer who impersonated an ancient confederate widow (*Oldest Living Confederate Widow Tells All* by Allan Gurganus). Have women been afraid to write about aging because we are not supposed to age, or is there another reason? Of course, until the twentieth century, the old, old woman was a rarity because of the dangers of pregnancy and childbirth. We cannot pass over this too quickly. Charlotte Brontë, for example, died of complications of pregnancy—possibly toxemia. It's hard to know how many great women writers were lost that way. Among the child-free, there were other complications—self censorship, for example, even among the greatest.

I've often thought that Marguerite Yourcenar might have attempted the mock memoir of an aged Roman female rather than writing so beautifully of a fictional Hadrian in *Hadrian's Memoirs*, but she herself tells us why this would have been futile: "Another thing virtually impossible, to take a feminine character as a central figure . . . women's lives are much too limited or else too secret. If a woman does recount her own life, she is promptly reproached for no longer being truly feminine."

Yourcenar wrote this in the 1950s—a time when many women writers felt this way. I certainly did when I began to write seriously in the late sixties. I felt that a man's life had more weight, more gravitas, than a woman's. I also noticed that impersonating a male character was more likely to win praise for a woman writer. I even began writing fiction with a Nabokovian novel from the point of view of a mad male poet. But I never published it. "Too limited or else too secret," she says.

These days, women's lives are far from limited, though they are sometimes secret—because women can't reveal their transgressiveness. For many centuries, gay women concealed their deep friendships and their partners. There was always the fear of shocking families, not to mention critics who acted like reproving parents. When critics reinforce familial judgments, the writer feels particularly pained. And critics often do this.

I wanted to change this fear of female rebellion. I wanted to erase the secrecy of women's lives. Will I now find the courage to break the final taboo for women—being old? Now that feminine taboos are being smashed, can we acknowledge the old woman as a source?

This is a vexed question. A publisher once told me that there had never been a best seller about a woman over forty, forgetting *Mrs. Dalloway*. And though nobody would say this now, they would probably think it. This rule did not apply to Allan Gurganus, of course, but it undoubtedly has influenced the response of publishers to women's books—always looked at more critically unless they hew to a particular popular genre.

Few women writers have failed to experience the odd phenomenon of having their books criticized as if the books themselves were women. Ever since a nineteenth-century reviewer responded to *Jane Eyre* as if she were applying for a position as a governess and was found unsuitable, women's books have been subject to the same stereotypes that infuriate us as women. Sexual books are treated like sluts, even—or especially—by women reviewers. This would be funny if it did not scare away those very readers who might find the book enlightening. Male writers rarely receive criticism of that sort when they claim women's lives as their subject. In fact, they are praised for their empathy. Note the praise of Jonathan Franzen for *Freedom* and Jeffrey Eugenides for *The Marriage Plot*. Women's lives and bodies are supposed to be the subject for male artists. Because we are thought to be the emotional gender, from Flaubert and Tolstoy to Franzen and Eugenides, this remains true. Men find that writing about us enables them to deal with forbidden feelings. When we write about women's lives, we are thought to be doing something easy and obvious. When men do it, they are exercising "negative capability."

It's hardly easy to write honestly about women whether the writer is male or female. It's hardly easy to write honestly about *anything*. But women characters can present a minefield for women writers, because readers and critics think they know about women. Women are common property and regularly categorized—virgins, sluts, witches, crones. The best writers understand that categories won't wash, but even some of the greatest novelists like Flaubert and Tolstoy, for example, report that they had to write and rewrite *Madame Bovary* and *Anna Karenina* in order to get away from perceived stereotypes of women.

Stereotypes can be a trap for women writers as well, but at least we have our own ambivalence to fall back on. We are less likely to stereotype our own gender. But old? Being old is still taboo. In classic books by women, most protagonists are children or young adults. This remains true from Louisa May Alcott to Edith Wharton to Harper Lee.

Virginia Woolf, before her suicide, began the exploration of older women—like Mrs. Dalloway, who is in her fifties. Some writers look back on childhood from middle age—Zora Neale Hurston is an example. But an old protagonist looking back is rare. Will this change in the twenty-first century? Perhaps. It's too soon to know. Are women still interesting, even to other women, once we are no longer romantic heroines? That remains unknown. New is sexy. Old is not.

Even my brilliant four-year-old granddaughter, Bette, will discover all this soon enough. Perhaps the joy of being four is that she doesn't yet have a clear idea of age and the changes it brings. She has many people who are older than she is— her mother and I and her other grandmothers are ancient to her. Bette's friends are mostly her age. Her big brother is eight, which is older, not old. Her uncles are older but fun. And all those other grandparents are, well, old like me.

My questions to myself about writing are way too early for Bette to contemplate. But when she is middle-aged and I am gone, she may read my thoughts again and see what she thinks and feels. By then, all the definitions of old may have changed. I really hope so for her sake. Women are living longer and longer, and we should be valuable at any age.

Ursula Le Guin wrote that grandmothers would make the best explorers of outer space, as they are the only people who have truly "experienced, accepted, and acted the entire human condition." Our bearing and rearing done, our kids and grand-kids independent, our curiosity endless, we could explore the universe. "Into the spaceship, granny," she wrote. I used to agree with this fanciful notion, but now I think our grand-children need us to stay here on earth, show them how to be old—really old.

During the period I have been writing and rewriting this essay, my mother has died. She passed from this life peacefully after nearly one hundred and one years on the planet. I waited to see them wrap her and take her frail bones down from the bed she had not left for days. Hundreds of drawings, paintings, designs, three daughters, nine grandchildren, and seventeen great-grandchildren were her legacy. In the last few days, she was alert enough to respond to color, though she could not speak. I came to realize that I had underestimated her grasp of language. Color was her language, and a bright shirt I wore to sit by her side and tell her I loved her evoked a passion-ate response. Her passing has changed me more deeply than I would have thought.

I want to learn to break the taboo of old and make poetry of it.

DYING IS NOT BLACK
Touch, words, color,
my expiring mother
notices the red & purple of my shirt
with delight.

Color is her language
though she taught me
both painting & poetry

interlocking languages for her
& now for me.

She has no words for my shirt
but exclaims nonsense syllables
of joy, her only brush now
for the ecstasy of red,
the blue note
of mauve over it,
making plum.

Her sounds become
a damson jam
like her mother's,
sweet but muddled.
But her love is clear.

Her love assails
my eyes
as if it were
blood glittering
on a knife
aiming for
my heart.

MARILYN KRYSL

PASSING IT ON

I began to write at age four, and my first language was the rich, juicy King James Bible as declaimed by my grandmother. This book housed many voices: the prophets' scary warnings, Solomon's love songs, the Psalms' supplications, the chanting lineages, the high drama of Revelation's looming catastrophes—these exotic ways of speaking wafted through the air, thrilling me. Many waters cannot quench love, neither can the floods drown it: those lines fed me robust confidence.

I took the words into my mouth, tasted the voices, swallowed them. Words made music to listen to, dance to, rock myself to, and I learned to draw a picture of each word: a thing called "writing." I became that child phenomenon, a "big reader." I was in fourth grade when I carried the biggest book I'd ever seen to the librarian. *War and Peace,* she told me, was for grownups. I got my mother to check it out.

I remember a gestalt of moments as I sat on our porch swing, reading. The swing swung slower until it stopped, but I kept reading. When the paragraph ended, I waited, in a pause.

I was living the nuanced life of the imagination, a secret life of words in books, words that told stories, words that sang poems. And this life of words was thrilling. Books offered models of protagonists overcoming doubt. I believed that words would feed me, harbor me, and, if I were in danger, words would save me. I was experiencing my first and deepest love affair.

The swing swung slower and slower, and in those moments it occurred to me that I was extremely lucky, because I was capable of learning just about anything. The world was vast—*War and Peace* was proof of this—and my parents read only the newspaper. I loved them, but their lives seemed tiny and circumscribed, whereas I was expanding, learning things they might never know. In those moments I felt myself separate from them. They would accomplish what they could, but my path would diverge from theirs and sweep me far from them. I had complete confidence that I would go off into beautiful vastness, and whatever I did would reverberate through the world.

While I was finishing *War and Peace,* I came down with the mumps. I passed the time in bed reading, but when the swelling subsided and I came to the novel's end, I couldn't hear in my left ear. Saturdays my mother worked in her beauty shop, so my father drove me to visit a specialist in Wichita.

We rode the elevator up. The specialist wore a fiercely white coat. I put on headphones, and he told me to press the button on the chair arm when I heard a sound. I pressed when I heard a sound, and I pressed when I thought maybe I heard a sound. After the test, the specialist looked over my head and addressed my father.

"The nerve that translates sound waves into hearing is dead," he said. "And a hearing aid won't help because there's no way to fix a dead nerve."

My sense of myself as whole was heat dispersing through a grate. A tear slid down my cheek, and my father and I stepped into the elevator and descended. He seemed not to notice my tears. We walked out into sunlight.

"We'll eat in that restaurant across the street."

It was the fifties. No one in Kansas had heard of Freud and Jung. I ordered mashed potatoes, my favorite food, and tried to stop crying. My father gazed around the restaurant, staring over my head. *God is present at the point where the eyes of those who give and those who receive meet,* Simone Weil wrote. How could my father not notice my sadness? I needed comforting, and the word *love* was available, but he went on as though nothing out of the ordinary had happened. I fantasized that he too had a hidden wound, not in his ear but his heart. His heart had gone deaf and could not hear my grief.

We drove home, and my father told my mother the specialist's verdict.

"Oh you poor thing," she said, and hugged me.

Now I was angry. I was not poor, nor was I merely a thing. I was a hurt girl who had lost part of her body forever.

My grandmother tried to comfort me. "God still loves you," she said.

What good was God? He did not have a body.

I climbed the hill to my grandmother's pasture dotted with buttercups, and lay on my back beneath the endless sky of Kansas. Sun sent down its praise for all things. Indian paintbrush bloomed, and the earth beneath me was warm. The world was constantly constructing itself, each new leaf, each sound, each bit of light offering itself to the whole—and then what had been whole began to dry up, fade, disintegrate, disappear. But my wound wasn't like a skinned knee. It would not heal. I would carry this bit of deadness with me for the rest of my life.

In science class I'd had to build a model of an atom's nucleus and circling electrons. I thought about these invisible bits earth was made of, and I felt the sun's heat warming me. In the only way they could, the sun and the Great Lap of the land were comforting me. There were the whole and there were the wounded, and the whole and the broken were designed for each other.

I had had my first true lesson in humility.

I lay a long time in the sun-warmed grass contemplating the finality of all things.

The loss of part of my body made me stronger, and softer. Now I recognized the other wounded. In a crowd I saw the woman whose husband beats her, the boy who on his eighteenth birthday will hang himself in his parent's basement. We wounded ones were a tribe, and I went on through the dangerous world, and grew fat with love. My task, from then on, I knew, was to walk among the thin ones, the slashed ones, the cracked and broken ones, and give them water. Thus I became a quiet, confident, and unobtrusive healer.

During my hours of mysterious quiet, I discovered I wasn't that noun "a writer." Rather I was a verb: writing. The *Atlantic*, the *Nation* and the *New Republic* published my poems, and I began to teach writing at the University of Colorado at Boulder. I discovered that many students signed up for a writing course because, like me, they'd been wounded. Some came from families in which one parent, or both, were alcoholics, or inept at parenting. Others had been wounded by the world, as I had been. They needed to speak their pain, as I did mine. So I began to teach them. Though I was officially a professor, unofficially I was a healer. Writing and teaching writing were two of the ways I could help the young wounded heal.

When Dr. Jean Watson, head of the University's School of Nursing, established the Center for Human Caring and offered me a commission to write poetry about nurses, I didn't hesitate. She sensed that she could use the arts to describe and advance the work nurses do. Only the arts, she believed, would reveal the great reservoir of caregivers' invisible but vital and necessary expertise.

How fitting that I who had suffered a physical wounding would be invited to write about others who'd been wounded, and about the relation of these wounded to their caregivers. I had found a situation—or it had found me—where I could be of use. A year later the poems were collected in *Midwife*, published by the National League for Nursing and adopted as a textbook in nursing schools.

I'd reflected nurses' experience back to them, a gift they couldn't give themselves, and my portraits of these patient, generous beings were crucial validation of their wisdom.

I decided that I would continue to teach writing, but I would not seal myself inside the university's safe shelter. I began occasionally to take a semester's leave without pay, and go where I could be of service. When I chanced on a TV documentary about Mother Teresa's Kalighat Home for the Destitute and

Dying in Calcutta, I decided to volunteer. Working among Kalighat's destitute, wounded women turned out to be the wisest thing I could have done. I came away from the suffering I'd witnessed stretched, humbled, and vastly enlarged.

Later I volunteered in Sri Lanka as an unarmed bodyguard for an NGO called Peace Brigades International. The great majority of human rights activists were women members of the Mothers' Front, a grassroots group that organized antigovernment demonstrations and petitioned the government to release missing husbands, fathers, and children. The head of the Front was a physician, Dr. Saravanamuttu, whose son, Richard, a playwright and popular TV news anchor, had been kidnapped by a death squad. Because being an American had leverage here, my presence acted as a shield. And at the same time, I received the gift of observing brave, frightened Sri Lankans, modeling for me their courage to challenge their government.

The wounds of inequality may be the most devastating of all. Even those who are victims of injustice sometimes comfort themselves by suppressing their knowledge of injustice against them.

During the seventies, eighties and nineties many women scholars and writers seized the opportunity to claim inequality as their subject matter. I was one of those who built influential careers by exploring gender equality, and there were occasions when my satire of gender roles rankled some men. One writer in my department protested that the title of my short story collection *How to Accommodate Men* was offensive. I explained that the story was a harsh satire on both the male and female protagonists. I explained that I'd intended to call the book *Eating God* after a story in the collection, but my editor at Coffee House Press, Allan Kornblum, urged me not to, on grounds that *Eating God* might puzzle or offend readers from religious backgrounds. It was he who urged me to go with the title *How to Accommodate Men*, and when the issue of women's right to equal pay for equal work became an issue at the University of Colorado, I had Kornblum's enthusiastic support.

In a milieu where the humanities were often underfunded, conflicts over salaries were inevitable, and over the course of a decade, women profs at Colorado urged the administration to carry out a salary study. Finally, when administrators failed to act, women profs appealed to the media, and when the media aired details of our campaign for equal pay, administrators agreed to launch the study. Each woman who wanted to appeal chose three male profs whose careers paralleled hers and submitted the three vitae along with hers. Two of my matches were male fiction writers, and the third was my husband, a poet and nonfiction writer. It turned out that my case was one of the most egregious on the Boulder campus, and I was awarded a $12,000 raise and $36,000 in back pay. Because the administration's inequity came to the public's attention, the university would henceforth be obliged to act on women's complaints.

As a woman writer trying to make a living, I was necessarily "up against" men. But I'd had two advantages. One was my feisty mother, a model of "just do it" long before "just do it" gained fame. When as a child I said I had nothing to do, she corrected me. "The world is full of things to do," she said. "Build cities. Tame rivers. For starters you can take out the trash."

My second advantage was my loving grandmother and her Bible's rich speech. I'd swum in her sea of biblical language, sailed ancient and contemporary oceans of English lit—and allied myself to Art—which, as Joyce Carol Oates once said, *is a record of the artist explaining something to herself.*

In France the expression "women of a certain age" refers to "middle-aged" women who've raised children but still have erotic "flare." No doubt there are such women, but I am no longer one of them. In *How to Accommodate Men* one of my characters remarks:

> My neck has started to sag. I used to think of this part of me as my throat, and an asset. It came to the fore when-ever I threw back my head, and I threw back my head a lot then, flinging my long hair aside and striding on. Now this part of my anatomy resembles the national debt. Nor do I think of it as my throat. It's my neck, and there's nothing romantic about it. . . .
>
> It used to be that when I walked into a room the air spruced up. . . . Young men . . . congregated, offering me hors d'oeuvres. . . . Now when I walk into a room the air has been spruced up by one of those young girls with spiked hair. . . . Young men notice me only at the checkout counter. They want to know if I'd like paper or plastic.

Now I accept my wrecked neck and the loss of my once pert derriere. I rejoice that I've been allowed to keep my slender-ness, my shapely legs, and fab ankles. So my face is amassing grooves and sags? All great achievements, Maya Angelou tells us, require time.

I was the first of the five in my women writers' group to turn seventy. The other four resembled sleek, red cars on a racing course, revving their engines, aching for the starting flag so they could blindside me with compliments. They meant well by insisting that I didn't look nearly as old as I was.

Please, I said, correcting them. Please notice my wrinkles. They are hard-won proof of my diligence, my timidity, and my courage, of my fearful hesitation and my determination to go on and do it anyway. I told them about the day a teacher and excited preschool kids arrived at the bus stop where I waited. A boy climbed onto the bench beside me and looked up, studying my face. I looked down, studying his.

"You look really, really old," he said.

He spoke in awe, a young man who understood that the scars of our journey down the path of longevity were cause for wonder.

"You hairy impertinent bag of water," Alicia Ostriker writes in *The Book of Seventy*. "Now go dance / with the skeletons, . . . / that worm there is hungry . . ."

I like her honesty. And I stand far back and assess. Being female can be difficult when circumstances surrounding us are difficult, but at this late phase in my life, being female isn't the most crucial issue. Nor is being wounded my most prominent feature. I suspect that everyone is doing the best he or she can, given their circumstances, circumstances that continuously morph and change. I think of the porch swing where I'd held *War and Peace* in my hands. I will carry my love torch for words as long as they offer themselves, but already I'm losing language, words flaking off like hundreds of bits of dead skin. Bit by bit my "career," my "reputation," my "triumphs" and my "failures" fall away. Already I feel like one of the flame tree's hot, red blossoms opening, falling, wilting, and disappearing into the beautiful nothing/everything.

I will disappear. And before that happens, I've found a photograph of the person I'd like to resemble: Avedon's portrait of Isak Dinesen. The finest of lines texture her forehead, cheeks, chin. But it's her eyes that tell us that she's not weary. What might have become disillusionment has turned to wisdom. Her eyes reveal quiet, confident love streaming into the eyes of the beholder. Here, she seems to say, take great handfuls of this free love that's everywhere around you. Eat it by great mouthfuls until you're full. Then offer it around. Keep passing it on.

MAXINE KUMIN

METAMORPHOSIS: FROM LIGHT VERSE
TO THE POETRY OF WITNESS

How did I become a very old poet, and a polemicist at that? In the *Writer's Chronicle* of December 2010 I described myself as largely self-educated. In an era before creative writing classes became a staple of the college curriculum, I was "piecemeal poetry literate"—in love with Gerard Manley Hopkins and A. E. Housman, an omnivorous reader across the centuries of John Donne and George Herbert, Randall Jarrell, and T. S. Eliot. I wrote at least a hundred lugubrious romantic poems. One, I remember, began

> When lonely on an August night I lie
> Wide-eyed beneath the mysteries of space
> And watch unnumbered pricks of dew-starred sky
> Silent drop past the earth with quiet grace . . .

Deep down I longed to be one of the tribe, but I had no sense of how to go about gaining entry. I had already achieved fame in the narrow confines of my family for little ditties celebrating birthdays and other occasions, but I did not find this satisfying. There were no MFAs in poetry that I knew of except for the famous Iowa Writers' Workshop, founded in 1936; certainly there was nothing accessible to a mother of two, pregnant with her third child in 1953 in Newton, Massachusetts. I have noted elsewhere that I chafed against the domesticity in which I found myself. I had a good marriage, and our two little girls were joyous elements in it. But my discontent was palpable; I did not yet know that a quiet revolution in thinking was taking place. Of course motherhood was not enough. Perhaps I could become a literary critic?

Hoping to find direction, I subscribed to the *Writer*, a Boston magazine. There I found my destiny in an advertisement for Richard Armour's *Writing Light Verse*, $3.95. I would begin there, and if I hadn't published anything by the time this baby was born, I would turn my back on the Muse forever. My first ever four-liner appeared in the *Christian Science Monitor* in March of that year. When the check for five dollars came, I had recovered my investment in Armour's book, and had broken into print with this:

There never blows so red the rose,
So sound the round tomato
As March's catalogues disclose
And yearly I fall prey to.

I had been ghostwriting articles for some local doctors on subjects ranging from the benefits of electroshock to the treatment of third-degree burns, spending Saturdays at a medical library in Boston while my husband took over my domestic role. Now I had found a profession that was infinitely portable. I could try out lines in my head while doing the dishes or hanging the laundry—no dishwasher, no dryer—or conveying a child to a music lesson or the dentist. I grew adept at composing in the car while I waited for the musician or patient to be trained or treated. Here is one I've dredged up from my memory bank:

People who sleep like a baby
Don't mean what they say. Or maybe
They have no scions who wake
At midnight with ill-defined ache.
Nor have they at 2 yet another
child bringing her nightmare to Mother.
No indeed. If they had, they would gather
That this simile is mere blather.
As for me, I am happy to own up
I would much rather sleep like a grown-up.

Before long, I was being published in the pages of the *Wall Street Journal* and the *New York Herald Tribune*, and I was frequently appearing in the *Christian Science Monitor*. I also won acceptance in the *Ladies' Home Journal* and the *Saturday Evening Post*, among the leading magazines of the time. "Lines on a Half-Painted House" appeared in the *Post* in 1955:

In summer, beach and billows beckon;
And in between, you dab a speck on.
In autumn, who feels dutiful?
The foliage is beautiful.
In winter, little can be done;

The brush will freeze, the nose will run.
Spring's the time! The perfect instant!
And fortunately, two months distant.

About these lines I must add this incredible detail: my husband was required to provide a letter from his employer certifying that my poem was original. This is not as far-fetched as it sounds today. In the fifties, women, along with people of color, were still thought to be intellectually inferior, mere appendages in the world of belles lettres.

Writing light verse actually served me well as a poet. It pressed me into the exactitude of rhyme, and working in rhyme allowed me to trot some of my dark poems out of the closet and try to cast them in formal patterns. I greatly admired Edna St. Vincent Millay's sonnets, especially her skillful Petrarchan ones, all but unmatched to this day; W. H. Auden's deft tetrameter also pointed me forward.

I continued to write in isolation until 1957, when I stumbled upon a poetry workshop at the Boston Center for Adult Education conducted by the poet and Tufts University professor John Holmes. Anne Sexton and I met in that class; our deep personal and professional relationship ensued and ran for seventeen years until she took her own life. Holmes became my mentor, and in private I called him my Christian academic daddy. He proposed me for membership in the New England Poetry Club and soon thereafter put me up for my first academic position at his university.

Still, entry into this circle of emerging poets only highlighted the tension I felt at having to juggle domestic and professional spheres. This acrobatic act dominates a letter I wrote to my mother in 1958 to wish her a belated happy birthday:

> Just call me Mrs. Pepys. Up sooner than betimes; dryer broken, youngest out of underpants. All underpants soaking wet on line. Pouring. Ten minutes of earnest persuasion, no one would know he was wearing old baby pair, no one would see. Find plastic bag to protect violin case. (Pouring harder.) Write check for violin teacher. Overdrawn? Live dangerously; payday Wednesday. Find cough drops for middle child. Middle child coughs anyhow. Girls depart. Youngest watching Captain Kangaroo. Make beds, do dishes, get dressed; car pool late for youngest, writer late for appointment. Car pool comes, writer leaves; rushes to Tufts. Interview with chairman of English Department, 30 minutes. Consults my resume. What was Slavic course you took junior year? Think back; possibly 19th century Russian history. Discuss elements of English renaissance? Writer knows little about this period. Bluff. Next meet chairman, Freshman English. Amiable. Each have a cigarette. Back to chair of department. Accompany him across campus (still pouring) to meet Dean. Dean looks too young to shave. Has five children. Further discussion. Money not mentioned. Interview over. Decision after June 16. Arrive home, gobble sandwich, deliver girls back to school. Go pick up youngest, rush to bank for cash. Overdrawn? Live dangerously. At bank, youngest's stomach feels squirmy. Suspicious green tint to complexion. Throw up? Abandon plan to go to market. Rush

home. No temperature. Does not throw up. Borrow neighbor in case; go to market. Husband's sales director coming for dinner. Husband has clean shirt? Whiskey sours? No rye. Can't find noodle pudding recipe. Find it. Make pudding. Girl Scout cookout postponed, rain. Stops raining. Clean chicken, set table. Middle child comes home. Cello case? Lost. Found. Deliver middle child and cello to lesson. Home. Toss salad. Start children's dinner. Retrieve child and cello from lesson. Poets from workshop call, farewell party for John Holmes Friday night? Bake cake? Tomorrow. Find children for early supper. Throw on dress; husband and sales director arrive. Drinks. Dinner. Children to bed. Guest leaves and so betimes to bed.

I remember that life well. I was just beginning to get my "true" poems published, first in little magazines like *Audience* and the *Beloit Poetry Journal*, then acceptances from the *Atlantic*, *Harper's*, even the *New Yorker*. I remember teaching freshman comp part-time to phys-ed majors and dental technicians; I was the first woman ever hired in the Tufts University English department and therefore not to be trusted with liberal arts students.

Coming of age as a poet in the late 1950s and well into the '60s, I was not unconscious of the disdain with which aspiring women poets—and people of color—were treated. Gradually I came to realize how arduous the road to acceptance as a woman artist would be. Attitudes changed at a glacial pace. I have cited elsewhere, more than once, an event that took place in 1967. At a dinner hosted by the Poetry Society of America, Robert Lowell rose to praise Marianne Moore as the nation's best *woman* poet. Blessedly, Langston Hughes leapt up to assert that she was the best *Negro woman* poet in the country. What astonishes me is how few women today, hearing this story, appreciate the irony in it. Was she black? they ask.

In 1961, when my first book appeared, it was one of forty-odd poetry collections published in the United States that year. Just eight were by women. (That statistic and the following ones are provided by Wikipedia.) By 2011, the major trade publishers, independent presses, university presses, online publishers, even self-publish presses, had engorged that number and Wikipedia no longer listed them all, instead posting only the eighty-some poets chosen for David Lehman's annual *Best American Poetry* anthology. By my rough count, thirty-plus were women. This year (2012), Bill Henderson's Pushcart anthology processed approximately eight thousand poems that had been nominated for a prize by contributing editors and assorted journals. It seems safe to say that poetry, in all its permutations from rap lyrics to *sonnets redoublés*, is flourishing.

Holding one's first published collection of poems is matched only by the thrill of holding one's newborn child for the first time. I could hardly believe my good fortune. In 1961, the same year that *Halfway* came out, the Radcliffe Institute for Independent Study announced the recipients of its largess. Incredibly, both Anne Sexton and I were among the twenty-four women who received grants in fields ranging from poetry and painting to science, history, and philosophy. Although the dollar amounts were small, the grants authenticated us. They said we were real and what we did was valuable.

The Radcliffe Institute's validation freed me to see myself as a writer. Although poetry was my first and remains my most enduring love, I wrote extensively in other genres. I never felt any ambivalence about working in prose; in a comforting way it relieved the tension of the high-wire act of writing the poem. When my children were small I turned to writing stories for them, many in tight rhyme. Richard Wilbur, Jarrell, and Eliot had sanctified this terrain before me, and I found it joyful and relaxing. Now, only a handful of my twenty-five children's books remain in print; all five novels, my memoir, and my one collection of short stories are out of print; as far as I can tell, my four essay collections are still available.

In the midsixties, John Ciardi, director of the Bread Loaf Writers' Conference in Middlebury, Vermont, offered me a coveted position as a fellow. I declined, citing some bogus reason; the truth was I was too scared to accept. The prospect of rubbing elbows with a faculty of prominent writers paralyzed me. Luckily, Ciardi persevered. In 1969, when he invited me to join the Bread Loaf staff, I screwed up my courage and agreed. The experience was exhilarating, the atmosphere relaxed and friendly. I went back five more times.

When my fourth poetry book, *Up Country: Poems of New England*, won the Pulitzer Prize in 1973, I was stunned. The news came in a phone call from a local television station; I was certain someone was perpetrating a cruel hoax. Once I was persuaded the award was real, I was aghast. Harper & Row were, too. In six weeks they managed to renew the print run and bring out a paperback edition as well. However, when my editor, accompanying me to my first reading at the 92nd Street Y in New York, announced cheerfully, "This should be fun. I've never been to a poetry reading before," I was so unsettled that I misplaced the carefully annotated list of poems I planned to read and had to choose as I went along.

That summer after the flurry of interviews, including appearances on TV, I fled from suburban Boston to our derelict former dairy farm in New Hampshire. Candide's advice to cultivate my garden helped center me. I was truly afraid I would never write again—but the poems came, as they always had, on their own terms, beginning in the most unexpected ways and demanding that I pay attention. What was also unexpected was the flow of invitations to give readings and teach at a wide array of colleges and universities. Before the Pulitzer, the only major invitation I had received was thanks to Howard Nemerov, who had recommended me to Centre College as visiting professor. Danville, Kentucky, was a venue more exotic than Paris or Rome would have been. After the Pulitzer, I was an adjunct professor at Columbia. Next came two Fannie Hurst Professorships in succession at Brandeis University in Waltham, Massachusetts, and Washington University in St. Louis.

The following year we sold our snug little Cape Cod colonial in Newton and moved to New Hampshire full time. To my surprise and frequent consternation, I was launched in the poetry business; Pobiz Farm became the name of the craggy, hilly, overgrown property we were bent on restoring, and where we had started to raise horses. I was a wage-earning poet and an amateur distance rider. Often, flying to gigs in faraway states, I took my lightweight synthetic saddle with me in its own case. When someone next to me at the baggage claim asked, "What's in there?" I replied, "A tuba." En route to various outposts in California or Missouri my seatmate invariably asked me, "What do you do?" I never said that I was a poet because experience had taught me the rejoinder would be, "That so? Ever published anything?" I learned to say, "We raise horses," which was true and ate up much of my income.

Poetry and horses, with long days of labor (some of it hired but mostly our own) to reclaim cow pastures from the second-growth forest, dig postholes, and put up wooden fences, sand and repair or replace ancient clapboards. Along with the sprucing up, the books of poems accrued, a new one every three to four years. I left Harper & Row for Viking in 1975 (who needed an editor who had never been to a poetry reading?), then left Viking after the decision was made in 1989 to use the photo of a glossy Bambi-like fawn on the cover of *Nurture* instead of what I had lobbied for: a tiny kangaroo joey held against the immense scale of a human hand.

W. W. Norton became my publisher and Carol Houck Smith my editor. We did eight books together, one of them a collection of essays and stories, and each graced by a Wolf Kahn painting. I remember with particular fondness the afternoon we spent with a manuscript spread out on the double bed of my cramped room in the old Gramercy Park Hotel as we bumped our way around deciding which poems went with which others. Then Carol said, "Shall we go see Wolfie?" and we made our way several blocks uptown to the gallery and chose one of his glorious landscapes. Once I had been a suburban matron. Now I had lived so long in the country that I was skittish walking in the rush-hour crowds of pedestrians and crossing streets where impatient taxi drivers honked and gestured. Diminutive Carol asked, "Would you like me to hold your hand?" Looking down at her, I said, "Yes, please."

I was never comfortable in New York City; the canyons between skyscrapers felt ominous. By contrast, Washington,

DC, with its height limit on buildings, seemed airier, greener, less hectic. As the newly appointed 1981–1982 Poetry Consultant to the Library of Congress (a position renamed Poet Laureate four years later), I was able to select several women poets to read in a monthly series. Best known among them was Adrienne Rich, who had rejected previous requests from male laureates; that day, the line for admittance to the auditorium stretched around the block. I also instituted weekly brown bag lunches in the august Poetry Room, little used except for formally welcoming foreign poets. If my tenure is to be remembered for anything, let it be for those Thursday lunches where well-known writers brought their students or disciples for a noon gathering that often stretched to 4:00 p.m.

In 1995 I was appointed a chancellor of the Academy of American Poets alongside Carolyn Kizer. Together we lobbied for the appointment of the black poet Lucille Clifton to fill vacant posts, but twice we saw the positions go to white men. In November 1998 we resigned in protest, which ultimately led to the restructuring of the board: no longer could chancellors serve two consecutive twelve-year terms, and women and minorities achieved representation. We were praised by many and damned by a procrustean few.

Over the years many of my poems were rooted in the rural landscape; this led to my receiving the jocular epithet Roberta Frost. I didn't disavow this, but I did feel that it marginalized my work. Still, when Denise Levertov, a poet I admired for her lyric voice, began to write fierce poems against the escalating involvement of American troops in Vietnam, I had worried that her polemic would somehow damage her extraordinary gift. (It did not.)

Looking back, I see that as early as 1972 I confronted ethical issues in my own poetry. In "Heaven as Anus" from that year, a poem attacked as pornographic by a major public figure, I seized on the US government's use of animals for experimentation. It opens with:

> In the Defense Department there is a shop
> where scientists sew the eyelids of rabbits open
> lest they blink in the scorch of a nuclear drop

and closes with these lines:

> It all ends at the hole. No words may enter
> the house of excrement. We will meet there
> as the sphincter of the good Lord opens wide
> and He takes us all inside.

In 1982, in "Lines Written in the Library of Congress after the Cleanth Brooks Lecture," I wrote about the relationship between poetry and history:

> Poetry
> makes nothing happen.
> It survives
> in the valley of its saying.
> Auden taught us that.
> . . . .
> New poets will lie on their backs

listening in the valley
making nothing happen
overhearing history
history time
personal identity
inching toward Armageddon.

For much of my poetic lifetime, my focus was on the natural world, untampered with and unromanticized. But the face of violence and human cruelty eventually broke through—perhaps abetted by the fact that I have a daughter who worked for thirty-two years for the United Nations Refugee Agency. Hence my anguished rant against the Bosnian war and its impact on civilians in the 1994 sonnet "Cross-Country Skiing," which doesn't abandon the natural world, but puts it in perspective:

I love to be lured under the outstretched wings
of hemlocks heavily snowed upon, the promise
of haven they hold seductively out of the wind
beckoning me to stoop under, tilt my face
to the brashest bits that sift through. Sequestered,
I think how in the grainy videos
of refugees, snow thick as flaking plaster
falls on their razed villages. Snow
forms a cunning scrim through which the ill-clad
bent under bundles of bedding and children appear
nicely muted, trudging slow motion to provide
a generic version of misery and terror
for those who may step out of their skis to sit
under hemlock wings in all-American quiet.

In the same vein, "Mulching" from 2007's *Still to Mow* talks of reading the headlines while spreading old newspapers between plants in the vegetable garden:

> prostrate before old suicide bombings, starvation,
> AIDS, earthquakes, the unforeseen tsunami,
> front-page photographs of lines of people
> with everything they own heaped on their heads,
> the rich assortment of birds trilling on all
> sides of my forest garden, the exhortations
> of commencement speakers at local colleges,
> the first torture revelations under my palms
> and I a helpless citizen of a country
> I used to love . . .

My disenchantment turned to fury as the war in Iraq gathered steam, with the appalling use of torture by the United States and its proxies, the legal maneuvering at Guantanamo, and more. Now, nearly sixty years after my first four lines of light verse were published in the *Christian Science Monitor*, I feel that my work has truly metamorphosed into the poetry of witness, though my political poems were wrung from me. Some, like "Red Tape and Kangaroo Courts" from the *Hudson Review* (2012), are in unrhymed sonnet form. One, "Entering Houses at Night," evolved as a villanelle; another, "What You Do," as a pantoum—both to be found in *Still to Mow* and then included in *Where I Live: New & Selected Poems 1999–2010* (2011). Thematically, these poems are linked by my despair at the monstrous contempt American officialdom has displayed for justice and morality in the years since the 9/11 attacks:

the list of things that are prohibited
in the camps is itself prohibited

. . . .

and capital cases are heard with no
capital defense attorneys allowed
(from **"Red Tape and Kangaroo Courts"**)

We went in punching kicking yelling out orders
in our language, not theirs.
(from **"Entering Houses at Night"**)

when you shackle them higher
are you still Christian
when you kill by crucifixion
(from **"What You Do"**)

Although metrics serve as a way of giving shape to my anger and enabling my poetry to voice moral outrage, some of my rants are in free verse. Whatever methods writers in all genres use, we have to bear witness, hew to our personal compass, and stand up to be counted. To paraphrase Auden in his prescient poem "September 1, 1939," all we have is a voice "to undo the folded lie." Today we have literally thousands of poets raising their anguished voices, not just in English, but in Arabic, Russian, Farsi, and a hundred other tongues. Are our poems succinct, stunning, intensely moving? Of course we hope they are. Do they change the course of elections, undo death penalties, pardon political prisoners, expose fraud and corruption? These are rhetorical questions, but the poetry of witness at least provides a living archive, exposing the folded lies.

*
HONOR MOORE

ON CERTAINTY

I can tell you, certainty came with writing, as did age, and that I am always more certain in the sun than I am on a gray day, no matter what the season. I can also tell you that the other night I was giving a reading in Iowa City, and I realized, as I entered the small bar on Gilbert Street, that I had been giving readings for forty years.

I remember the first professional poetry reading I ever gave: walking up the hill in the Berkshires, placing my poems on a giant stump of a long ago tree. Robert Creeley was reading with me, but he didn't read *with* me. He climbed the hill as I was finishing my last poem, staggering, drunk, and then read. Thirty-three years later, less than a year before he died, I met him for the first time—I didn't meet him the day of the reading—and told him about that day, him drunk and not there. It turned out he was kind. He listened and smiled: "I'll make it up to you," he said, making it up to me just by saying that.

My second reading took place in a dark room on East 73d Street. My hair was very long and my mother was there and my grandmother, my father's mother, both dead now. I read a poem called "My Mother's Moustache," an epic about the trials of facial hair. My grandmother said, "Your poems are too Elizabeth Arden. You should write about the moon."

I remember my first reading in a room full of women; thirty of us read, one of us had been a prostitute. After that, there were many readings in rooms full of women, women of all ages. I remember finding certainty in those rooms, certainty that I was writing as a woman, a fact that vastly expanded my possible material.

Once I read on the Staten Island Ferry and was not able to get my footing, and once I read the poem by Emma Lazarus, "Give me your tired, your poor" to a room full of old people at a Jewish nursing home and one of my listeners remembered steaming into New York harbor from Poland when she was a girl.

When my mother was dying, I wrote poems in a small notebook. I was twenty-seven and she was fifty. I remember the first reading I gave of those poems, how at last, because I was writing consciously as a woman, I could speak with depth and certainty about loving my mother and about something that had happened to me: "Do you know how, when you find out your mother has cancer and might die, how you feel at last legitimate?"

There was a time at a place called Calliope, a salon in Westbeth in downtown New York, when there were readings organized once a month by a woman called Ree Dragonette whom I considered old. She had short gray hair, a theater-trained voice, and wore long colorful caftans. When she announced a poet, she was a bit flirtatious. I remember thinking, she's too old to be flirtatious.

I am older, probably, than she was then and I flirt with certainty, often on the page.

The play I made from the poems about my mother's dying opened on Broadway just after my twenty-ninth birthday. I remember that I wore a green cape and stood in the lobby as people arrived on opening night, and I remember that when the telephone call came the next day to tell me the play was closing after a week of previews and one night, I was being interviewed by the *Washington Post* and the photographer snapped me in tears, one hand touching a handkerchief to my eye. The photo of me crying was huge and on the front page of the Style section, and I remember that my hand looked strange. I was crying for the loss of my mother, for the loss of my work, and for the loss of the certainty it had given me.

I did not know then that losing certainty was temporary.

It took months to get certain again. I wrote in a long flannel nightgown and had flu for days and days. I became certain by writing the next poem, and another kind of certain by putting my play in a book among other plays by women. I wrote a historical introduction about women playwrights and put myself among them.

I have read in a diner in Connecticut and at the Cathedral of St. John the Divine in an antinuclear concert. Twenty people in a diner was a big crowd, and so were five thousand in a cathedral.

I once read in a suburban Barnes and Noble during a hurricane. The audience was five people, and once I read in a prison in Indiana and, wearing a long black dress, in a ballroom in New York.

I am trying to explain how reading my poems gave me certainty, how ever since I began to write poems and read them aloud to others, I have had certainty. In writing I came to speak in a voice that had always been silent, giving new language to the voice that while silenced had always kept me uncertain.

There is an account in a book by H.D. of traveling with her partner Bryher and men often saying to them, Are you two women alone? I invented an idea for myself, The Romance of Alone. I was looking out the window waiting for my boyfriend to come home once, shaking with uncertainty. I imagined that if I fell in love with being alone, I would never have to shake again with that kind of uncertainty. I came to know that to some great degree, the life of a writer is a romance of alone, but also that when one writes, one is never alone.

I remember writing my first long book, how long I was alone.

I remember dreaming books whose pages are empty when I stand up to give a reading from those books. I dream that still.

I've read in a hotel in Florida and by candlelight in a place I cannot now remember.

I remember reading outdoors in the cold in Iowa, after a beautiful man danced nude.

I still read poems and pages on the phone to friends: Do you like this? Oh, do you like this?

I remember my friend from Austria, a woman my mother's age, saying in her accent, "You are a poet."

I remember hearing Muriel Rukeyser read months before she died at sixty-seven. *Sixty seven!!* I am sixty seven as I write this, and I thought she was old!

When I am old I will wear purple. . . . At supper with Adrienne Rich, I once met the poet who wrote that: Jenny Joseph. When asked by the greeting card company that first reprinted that poem if she would prefer a flat fee or royalties, she chose royalties, and that poem bought her a house. I have always worn purple, but now I hesitate. Will they think I wear it because I'm old? I wear black, often with orange, red, or deep pink.

I remember reading in a hot room on an island, how I sweated, and in a room at twilight on an island in Greece as the sun set. I have read at morning and at midnight and I have read Gertrude Stein on the radio, and once when we read poems from women of the past on the radio the singer Odetta, there by chance, joined us, reading the blues.

Not long ago I read in a park in New York City with a man I thought I was in love with. I remember after my mother's death reading a poem about my parents' separation that was not kind to my father, and that my father was in the room, sitting in the back. I remember reading with Sonia Sanchez and meeting her father and how proud he was of her.

My father said he was proud of me for reading what I believed to be the truth, but I never read that poem again and I withdrew it from publication. Now, as I write again about my mother, her life and her death, both of my parents are present, sitting in the back of my mind. I write about them to become certain about where it is they are sitting, about what their faces look like, about what their lives mean.

The other day, when I realized that I had been giving readings for forty years, the reading I was on my way to give was part of a Valentine's Day reading with students. Speakeasy Erotica, it was called. What will they make of me, I thought, this woman vastly older than they are, reading about bare skin, longing, and the call of the body?

At what age is one ever certain? To what age will I certainly live? And these words that I have written, will they live on?

✳

ALICIA OSTRIKER

SPLITTING OPEN: SOME POEMS ON AGING

1

There is so much to say about aging as a woman. Far too much. And most of it in tremendous need of being said. Remember Muriel Rukeyser's remark,

> What would happen if one woman told the truth about her life?
> The world would split open.

She was right, and the world is continuing to split, like atoms, releasing energy, as women speak previously unspeakable truths. I have written poems that touch this subject throughout my life. In a marriage poem in my first book I prayed:

> Let us become a toddling old couple.
> Let us make quaint appearance at weddings and funerals. . . .
> Let neither of us tend the other's cancer
> But race, for whose heart bursts first, his or mine.

I wasn't thirty when I wrote that, but my father had died of a heart attack and my father-in-law of cancer. It seems to me that my poems, far more than any analytic essay I could write, capture the emotions involved in struggles we all may endure. So let me follow one slender thread of poems into this labyrinth, looking at work responding to three age-related female crises: midlife, mastectomy, and the mandate of seventy.

First, some backstory. At thirty I stopped calling myself a girl and began calling myself a woman. At forty I started lecturing myself: if there's something you want to do with your life, get on your horse and do it. It was in my forties that I finally defined myself as a poet, not just someone who "teaches English." Fifty was more difficult. As fifty approached, a white fog descended around me so that I could not see where I was going, and everything in my life became questionable. I had just published *Stealing the Language* and a book of poems, *The Imaginary Lover,* that ended up winning the William Carlos Williams Prize. I had two daughters in college and a son in high school, a successful and supportive scientist husband, all of us in good health. I should have been a happy person, right? But no. The white fog blotted everything out. Who was I, what did I want to become? What would I do with my maternal instincts when my children left? Did I want to stay in my marriage? Would I ever write poetry again? Unable to imagine a future for myself, increasingly depressed and whining in the ear of my somewhat patient husband, I kept looking at older women for models: no, not that one, not that one, not that one . . .

And then one night I sat bolt upright in bed. I had it. My mother-in-law, Jeanne Ostriker, had been smart, good-looking, a tireless political campaigner (lefty Democrat of course), a master teacher of English in an at-risk public school. Jeanne was a fighter, disregarding doctor's advice to take it easy, right to the end, which took her at age sixty-five. I had loved her, she had loved me. She'd been gone two decades, and I still loved her. "Honey," I shook my husband awake.

"I've got my model. It's your mom."

He half opened his eyes. "Tell me if you still think so in the morning."

I did, and Grandma Jeanne lasted me a long long time, yet the white fog was the beginning, for me, of facing death— and defying it as best I could. In my book *Green Age*, which might well have been titled *The Book of Fifty*, the obsession is obvious. A poem called "George in Hospital" describes my dying stepfather with his voice "like traprock down a chute / the hunks of gravel grating against metal," yelling "Oh Mary and Jesus, this is terrible." A poem called "Helium" describes releasing my husband's birthday balloon when it grows old and puckered, watching it disappear behind a neighbor's copper beech, not knowing "if it was still ascending / or stopped in the arms of a tree," and being "glad of this" as a symbol of not knowing his destiny. One sequence of poems called "The Death Ghazals," meditates on ways to die, from Homer and Shakespeare to AIDS and a Middle East battlefield. The key poem of this book, simply entitled "Fifty," alludes to Gloria Steinem telling reporters "This is what a fifty-year old woman looks like," and attempts to probe past that bravado:

Do you think: *Let's keep this thing*
Rolling, keep on fighting, keep
Up the good work,
And glare down the steel tracks of the mirror

At the approach of the enemy
Who is still miles away
But coming like a commuter train, do you
Hit your typewriter
Every day, harder
And harder, like a recalcitrant
Spoiled child, have you surrendered
The hope of the perfect
Romance, or do you grip that
Fantasy stubbornly, like a kid holding
On to a dead pet
That she knows is dead
And do you make a joke of all of this
And when the clock says *Almost*
Quitting time, do you still answer *Never?*

A few things strike me in retrospect about this poem. I felt proud, at the time of writing, of holding my head high, fighting, identifying with a heroine like Gloria Steinem. Yet defiance—not going gently into that good night, as Dylan Thomas would say—could also be considered denial. What the poem accomplishes—what writing a poem *can* accomplish—is two contradictory things at once. Denial of fear and confession of fear coexist. The solvent is humor. Making "a joke of all of this" is a survival strategy and a strategy in poetry.

2

Green Age was published in 1989. Two years later, in late fall, a mammogram disclosed some spots. They looked like dust—dust thou art—but it turned out that they were tiny malignancies: ductal cancer in situ. Terror descended over me like a skin of ice. I had the mastectomy before the year was out, so that I would be able to return to teaching in spring semester. A confirmed workaholic, I have always found that keeping busy, keeping busy, keeping very busy, prevents trauma from infecting the entire organism. As Satchel Paige said, "Don't look back. Something may be gaining on you."

However, when it comes to healing, nothing beats poetry. Half a year after the mastectomy, I gave myself the gift of a solitary week in our little place in the Berkshires, where we have no electricity, no phone, nothing to interfere with a woman who wants, at last, to revisit her neglected inner self. I had two cartons of books, a portable radio, wine, a meadow, a pond, and June sunshine. I could skinny-dip. I could teach myself to caress my scar and tell my body I still loved it. I could relinquish control and cry if I wanted to. That week saw the beginning of many poems ultimately published in *The Crack in Everything*, including the twelve lyrics of "The Mastectomy Poems." As soon as those poems started to appear, I knew they would be no-holds-barred.

People ask if it wasn't difficult to write about mastectomy. Yes, difficult in the sense that I revised and polished those poems endlessly, scrupulously, pressing for the right word, right cadence, right metaphor, using the poems not simply to record what I remembered of the experience, but to discover what I didn't yet understand about its meaning. At the same time, I knew that these poems would, if I did my job well, be useful to other women. And so, writing these poems was a joy. I have always felt so lucky to be a poet—once I accepted this as my identity—because no matter how grim an experience may be, I can make something beautiful out of it. Particularly when a subject is taboo, breaking the taboo is a powerful and pleasurable challenge. "Write what you are afraid to write," I always tell my students. "Kill the censor." I like to quote Shostakovich's remark about his Thirteenth Symphony, dedicated to the Jews of Kiev massacred at Babi Yar in World War II, a massacre that was covered up until Yevtushenko wrote his famous poem about it. "Art destroys silence," said Shostakovich. And although breast cancer is no longer the taboo topic it was in 1990, the discourse around "breasts" remains either sanitized and simplified, or grossly eroticized. What I wanted in these poems was to tell the truth, the whole truth, which included technology, fantasy, sexuality, brutality, and (of course) ambiguity. Metaphor was essential. Here, for example, is the fifth poem in the series, a kind of elegy for "What Was Lost":

What fed my daughters, my son
Trickles of bliss,
My right guess, my true information,
What my husband sucked on
For decades, so that I thought
Myself safe, I thought love
Protected the breast.
What I admired myself, liking
To leave it naked, what I could
Soap and fondle in its bath, what tasted
The drunken airs of summer like a bear
Pawing a hive, half up a sycamore.
I'd let sun eyeball it, surf and lakewater
Reel wildly around it, the perfect fit,
The burst of praise. Lifting my chin
I'd stretch my arms to point it at people,

Show it off when I danced. I believed this pride
Would protect it. . . .

The poem's close changes tone:

Jug of star fluid, breakable cup—
Someone shoveled your good and bad crumbs
Together into a plastic container
Like wet sand at the beach
For breast tissue is like silicon.
And I imagined inland orange groves,
Each tree standing afire with solid citrus
Lanterns against the gleaming green,
Ready to be harvested and eaten.

Looking at this poem now, so many years later, I feel grateful that I was able to capture in the net of language, thanks to the power of metaphor, so much of the natural and the animal, the sensual and the moral, the aesthetic and the social meanings of my lost breast, meanings you would not find in medical or self-help texts. I am guessing that deep healing—which is not the same as "getting over it"—demands deep recognition of what has been lost. And what about "getting over it," which is what normal social interaction, after all, demands? The poem "Normal" evokes the hypocrisy of pretending that everything is "quite all right" after a mastectomy and how this chimes with so many surrounding hypocrisies, with the resentment the sick feel for the well, along with the sense that one has been attacked by some kind of alien creature and the ultimate sense of disgust one cannot help but internalize:

First classes, the sun is out, the darlings
Troop in, my colleagues
Tell me I look normal. I am normal.
The falsie on my left makes me
In a certain sense more perfectly normal.
An American who lives beyond my means,
A snake-oil foot in the door,
A politician with a strong
Handshake in an election year.

My scar, the poem goes on to say, is like an asp or a worm
that "would prefer to crawl off / Yet it is pink and smooth as
gelatin. . . . want to pet it?" The poem's close moves into the
surreal:

Now I am better, charming. I am well.
Yes, I am quite all right. I never say
The thing that is forbidden to say,
Piece of meat, piece of shit.
Cooled, cropped, I'm simple and pure.
Never invite my colleagues
To view it pickled in a Mason jar.

Is the irony here too heavy? Is the contrast between seeing the lost breast as something wonderful, and seeing it as a
"piece of meat, piece of shit," too stark? Is the personification
of the scar too weird? Is the animus toward my "normal" colleagues too unpleasant? Perhaps. Yet to deny the unpleasant-
ness would be to deny a significant portion of reality. It is not
enough to call oneself a survivor. Acknowledging the ongoing
darkness in oneself is part of being human. Finally, however,

life does go on. As Leonard Cohen says, "There is a crack, a crack in everything, / That's how the light gets in." The final poem in the series is called "Epilogue:"

> The bookbag on my back, I'm out the door.
> Winter turns to spring
> The way it does, and I buy dresses.
> A year later, it gets to where
> When they say *How are you feeling,*
> With that anxious look on their faces,
> And I start to tell them the latest
> About my love life or my kids' love lives,
> Or my vacation or my writer's block—
> It actually takes me a while
> To realize what they have in mind—
> *I'm fine,* I say, *I'm great, I'm clean.*
> The bookbag on my back, I have to run.

Questions remain. Am I running to classes, or home to make dinner, am I running to something fulfilling? Or just running away? I can't decide, can you?

3

Fast forward to age sixty-five, when my mother-in-law's guidance runs out, because she herself died at sixty-five, and my own mother dies after two years in an assisted living facility. I am on my own. *The Book of Seventy,* seventy pages in length, is a cross-section of who I am now. Less defiant, perhaps, more accepting. Or less in denial. Still healthy, though minus a breast, hair thinning, teeth unreliable, I find that mortality looms, and worse than mortality, the process of dying. I still pray for a heart attack. My greatest fear is that I won't be granted a swift termination by stroke or coronary but will be slowly and agonizingly reduced by Alzheimer's to a person without a mind; that my body will outlive my mind, that my mind will turn to mush and I'll have to watch it doing that.

The Book of Seventy, like all my collections of poetry, spreads its net wide. There are poems on family, on politics, on sexuality (yes, why not), on myth, on the cycles of nature. There are also poems dealing with the terror of aging. In these poems I feel, as with the mastectomy poems, that the less I censor myself, the more the poems will speak to others. Insomnia, for example, is not taken very seriously by this culture; it is serious, and it can open the door to a bleak but necessary clarity. The poem "Insomnia" shifts from a set of customary lacerating thoughts:

> you call yourself a coward
> you wake at 2 a.m. thinking *failure,*
> *fool,* unable to sleep, *unable to sleep*
>
> buzzing away on your mattress with two pillows
> and a quilt, *they call them comforters,*
> *which implies that comfort can be bought*
>
> *and paid for, to help with the fear, the failure*
> your two walnut chests of drawers snicker, the bookshelves mourn
> the art on the walls pities you, the man himself beside you
>
> asleep smelling like mushrooms and moss is a comfort
> but never enough, never, the ceiling fixture lightless. . . .

to what lies behind those thoughts:
you brag to friends you won't mind death only dying

what a liar you are—
all the other fears, of rejection, of physical pain,
of losing your mind, of losing your eyes,

they are all part of *this!*
Pawprints of *this!* Hair snarls in your comb
this glowing clock the single light in the room

One last poem, "At the Revelation Restaurant," takes its start from the inevitable self-pity a woman feels about her fading looks, her fading body. How not to be trapped in that self-pity? Laughing at oneself may help. Ecclesiastes, famous for the line "Vanity, vanity, all is vanity," in the King James translation of the Bible, is perfectly clear-eyed about the ultimate meaninglessness of all human activity, since everything ends in death, yet he advises us to eat, drink, and be merry—while we can:

Ecclesiastes sits across the table
and whenever I start to whine
he starts to laugh

sometimes so heartily and suddenly
that he spills his soup—

This actually cheers me up. Another ally for me is Mama Gaia, the earth mother herself. In my imagination, she flounces from the kitchen:

exclaiming, *Must we despise our bodies*
just because the philosophers and pharmaceuticals,

the priests and politicians, the advertising industry
and the movie industry tell us to?
so I whisper, Mama, I like my body

washing and touching itself in the bath
was the beginning, so sweet, then dancing
and kissing—too late to stop now—

since I know my eyeballs and clitoris
will turn to muck or dust as the Preacher
points out, and the process of dying

unless I am very lucky will be slow and painful,
Mama, tonight I intend to order
the soup, the salad, the entrée, the dessert.

When I look at this poem objectively, I see that my impulse to defy age, loss, and death is as strong now as it was when I was fifty. I am not ready yet to go gently into that good night.

LINDA PASTAN

OLD WOMAN, OR NEARLY SO MYSELF:
AN ESSAY IN POEMS

I was born a wrinkled, squalling baby, almost killing my mother in the process. Since she had an arduous recovery, even losing a rib to pneumonia, I spent the first six weeks of my life in an impersonal hospital nursery, returning home viscerally acquainted with loneliness and therefore, perhaps, old before my time. Maybe that's why I started writing poems and short essays about abandonment and death when I was barely twelve, though it was usually a deer or some other animal that had to die in my verse or prose. Maybe that's why I thought I knew what old age would be like, long before I actually reached it, identifying sometimes with my ancient-seeming grandmother, who was actually not so ancient at all. I was barely in my forties when I wrote:

OLD WOMAN
In the evening
my griefs come to me

one by one.
They tell me what I had hoped to forget.
They perch on my shoulders
like mourning doves.
They are the color
of light fading.

In the day
they come back
wearing disguises.
I rock and rock
in the warm amnesia of sun.
When my griefs sing to me
from the bright throats of thrushes
I sing back.

I didn't know much about griefs back then, and now that I am learning (parents, cousins, friends falling by the wayside), they certainly don't sing to me; the only rocking chair I own is the repository of clothes that I have not had time to hang up. But I still feel connected to this poem, possibly because sunlight is something that has always comforted me, and I often drag my chair from room to room, following the sun's path across the sky.

"Ethics" is the name of another poem I wrote in my forties, taking on the persona of an old woman. It is about the perennial question of what to do in a museum if a fire breaks out: should you save the Rembrandt painting or the old woman who is looking at it? The poem then moves from the abstract to the immediate:

This fall in a real museum I stand
before a real Rembrandt, old woman,
or nearly so, myself.

When I first read that poem aloud, I found myself involuntarily smiling when I came to those words "old woman / or nearly so, myself," for I was very far from being old then. As the years progressed, however, I had to stop smiling, for year after year of experiences—marriage, childbirth, the loss of many loved ones, had taken me far from that young girl in ethics class.

But now if I read the poem aloud, I smile again, this time because the "nearly so" is once again untrue: at eighty, I am indeed an old woman already. In this way I have been able to measure the passing of the years by the waxing and waning and waxing of that smile.

I eventually came to know what old age is really like and to document it in a variety of ways. The moment, for instance, when I realized I could no longer read names in the telephone book without holding it at arm's length (not to mention the fact that back then I did still use telephone books).

PRESBYOPIA
The eye
defects first—
or is it the world
which takes the first step
backwards?
No matter.
Those blurred numerals

on the page
are tracks
to be followed
the rest of the way
alone.

And then there is that most universal symptom of old age:
the inability to sleep through the night without several bathroom trips; the inability to fall back asleep once one has wak-
ened.

INSOMNIA

I remember when my body
was a friend,

when sleep like a good dog
came when summoned.

The door to the future
had not started to shut,

and lying on my back
between cold sheets

did not feel
like a rehearsal.

Now what light is left
comes up—a stain in the east,

and sleep, reluctant
as a busy doctor,

gives me a little
of its time.

Apart from the outward manifestations of age, the inner, psychological changes can be at least as damaging—plus the realization that, being among the elderly, we hold a different position in the world, in the family; that we are looked at differently even by our own children. And then there is that sweetly devastating moment when one of your children tries to take care of you, becoming in a sense the parent herself.

I believe this is particularly difficult for a woman like me who has never been in the workplace, has never had a real university affiliation, and whose only "place" is either sitting alone at her desk or in the constellation of the family (one husband, three children, seven grandchildren) she spent so many years creating. I don't think I was consciously thinking about all of this when I wrote "Sometimes." But I know now that I was already trying to come to terms with how things were changing, the way I always come to terms with things: by writing about them.

SOMETIMES
from the periphery
of the family
where I sit watching
my children and
my children's children

in all their bright
cacophony,

I seem to leave
my body—
plump effigy
of a woman, upright
on a chair—
and as I float
willingly away

toward the chill
silence of my own future,
their voices break
into the syllables
of strangers, to whom
with this real hand
I wave goodbye.

Perhaps only a woman, damaged in some ways by the culture in which she grew up, would have included the word "plump" in line 10. Ready to "willingly" embrace my own not too distant death, I am still conscious of wanting to weigh less, to have the kind of body Hollywood had taught me was proper. How true and how truly embarrassing.

But it is the consciousness of death coming closer and closer that has been under the surface not only of the poems I have included here but of so many of my poems from the very beginning—all those leaves falling, all those expulsions from Eden! Coming to terms with this on a personal level led me to a poem like "50 Years," a poem which at least in part has some perspective on age and approaching death. And in it, again, shines that all-important sunlight.

50 YEARS
Though we know
how it will end:
in grief and silence,
we go about our ordinary days
as if the acts of boiling an egg
or smoothing down a bed
were so small
they must be overlooked
by death. And perhaps

the few years left, sun drenched
but without grand purpose,
will somehow endure,
the way a portrait of lovers endures
radiant and true on the wall
of some obscure Dutch museum,
long after the names
of the artist and models
have disappeared.

There are some conditions of aging that are particularly hard for a writer, in fact for any kind of artist. Should we keep on working, even into extreme old age, if our work lacks the creative energy it used to have? If our own powers are fading, should we just stop? (Should Matisse not have made his paper cutouts simply because they are not as powerful as his paintings were?) I don't know the answer to these questions, nor can I compare my own recent work to my earlier work with an impartial eye. I try to remember the strong poems Stanley Kunitz wrote almost until the end. But the temptation to retire, as so many of my contemporaries are doing (from all sorts of professions, from teaching to playing the cello) is certainly there, and I speak of that (tongue only partly in cheek) in a poem called "Firing the Muse."

FIRING THE MUSE

I am giving up the muse Calliope.
I have told her to pack up her pens and her inks
and to take her lyrical smile,
her coaxing ways, back to Mt. Helicon,
or at least to New York.
I will even write her a reference if she likes
to someone whose head is still fizzy
with iambs and trochees,
someone still hungry for the scent of laurel,
the taste of fame, for the pure astonishment of seeing
her own words blaze up on the page.
Let me lie in this hammock in the fading sun
without guilt or longing, just a glass
of cold white wine in one hand,
not even a book in the other. A dog
will lie at my feet who can't read anyway,
loving me just for myself, and for
the biscuit I keep concealed in my pocket.

I have not given up the muse yet, nor do I intend to. Writing poetry is not something I choose to do; it is something I seem to have to do, for better and for worse. But I have certainly changed my writing habits. I no longer force myself to sit in my study all morning, every morning, as I did for so many years. Instead, when I turned sixty, I decided to try to write two poems a month, whenever and wherever I pleased. At seventy I decided one poem a month would be enough. At eighty? I'm not sure yet.

Crucially, I don't feel old inside. Does anyone? How grateful we all can be to that old friend Denial: I'm still surprised when I am given senior movie tickets without having to show ID. I'm still angry when people ask who colors my hair and are surprised when I tell them I never turned gray. Here then, to conclude, is a poem for all the women "of a certain age" who are grappling with so many of the issues I grapple with every day.

ANY WOMAN

I am neither the crinkled face
in the mirror nor the one
in the photograph, young
and frowning.
Sometimes I am the sleeper
who wakes and like Eve
thinks it is the first morning,
dew on all the silken surfaces
of the world.

Age has nothing to do with me.
Lust still raises its purple flag
and envy its green one—
don't I repent the same sins
every year, make the same resolutions?

When I was a child I had an old face,
and my mother who comforted me then
comforts me still
in her invisible arms.

Alone, I am any woman
fresh from the shower,
covering the newly rained upon
continent of her body—hills and valleys—
modestly with a towel.
Later, someone on the bus stands up
and offers his seat.
Who can it be for? I am
the only one standing.

＊

EDITH PEARLMAN

PUBLIC APPEARANCES

My first gig was in a bar. A little magazine, which died thereafter, thought that an early story of mine would entertain the
patrons. So I climbed onto a chair, and, unseen in the smoke
and inaudible in the din, declaimed to an audience who heard
nothing except the crack as one leg of the chair collapsed and
the thud as I was projected onto the chest of a very fat man.
One guy did clap—he thought it was part of the act.

My career as Literary Figure proceeded through the decades from unattended readings at bookstores, poorly attended
ones at libraries, better attended ones at writing conferences,
and one overflow crowd at a literary festival. At that festival I immediately preceded the headliner; all three hundred
people in the audience had come to hear David Sedaris. There
was excitement, I discovered, in speaking to a hushed house
in a darkened theater—even if the listeners were merely toler-
ating me, the forgettable opener.

These days, reading to reasonably large crowds, I have become confident, though a single cough can raise the fear that

the assembly, stricken *en masse* with bronchitis, will glide out one by one until I am left reading to the first cougher.

But my own voice is strong, my trousered stride steady, and I'm in moderate demand.

You can call this a kind of success. Brave and sober, I make Public Appearances. Never mind that Public is one of the most fearsome words in the language we employ, and Appearances is another. Public reminds us of our worst nightmare—not the venerable one of showing up on a stage with nothing on, but a new one of showing up on a stage with nothing to say. Appearances is what our mothers told us to keep up. The two words linked are toxic. To respond positively to an invitation to Appear in Public is the acme of masochism. Yet I do it—*we* do it, we writers. We say that it is a way to sell our latest book, or to meet our readers, or to keep our name alive (that name which, we predict, will soon require a morphine drip); or because everybody else does it. But except for some poets among us, we are not performers by preference; we write not to give a crowd something to listen to in an auditorium but to give an individual something to read in his easy chair.

Nevertheless, we Publicly Appear. We are willy-nilly part of the oral tradition, which can be likened to a chain letter whose first link was forged by Homer. Heaven forbid that we be the ones to break the chain. When we meet each other at parties or airports, we exchange the usual meaningless kiss and immediately complain about fatigue, muscle spasms in our smiling lips, hotel air conditioners that can be turned up but not down or off; and the fear that somewhere bedbugs are readying themselves for a little cuddle.

But there is something else within that keeps us going. That something is called, not to put too fine a point on it, ham.

Recently my agent received an invitation for me from a professor in a college in—oh, let us say Atlanta because it wasn't Atlanta. The professor wanted me to discuss my new book with her writing class, give a public reading, sign books for my fans, and dine with the luminaries of the university. As a side pleasure I could visit the famous museum of art and go to a baseball game. And I would be paid my usual honorarium, which has reached four figures (the original bar gave me a thimbleful of wine free; alas—I spilled it when the chair ousted me), and I'd be reimbursed for travel and accommodations.

The problem was: I didn't want to go to there, or anywhere. I wanted to remain fondling the keys of an old Hermes typewriter that sits on a desk in a small apartment looking out on a city park. I wanted to work on my current story and read other people's stories and listen, if it's the right day, to the cheers or groans of the fans at nearby Fenway Park. Alone.

Oh, don't be so elusive, said my inner voice. *Admit that you love praise and applause, the fulsome introduction and the stream of compliments, even the threat of amorous bedbugs.*

Homer may have been the first ham, but it was Dickens who raised hamminess to high-priced heights. On his reading tours he developed a new, composite art form, acting out specially adapted passages from his own works and varying his expressions and speech patterns. It seemed as if he were turning into the characters he created. His readings drew large audiences on both sides of the Atlantic, and probably contributed to his premature death from a stroke.

We follow not only Homer and Dickens but also a chorus

line of daring reformers—Emma Goldman, Victoria Claflin Woodhull, Jane Addams, to name a few. They spoke to huge popular acclaim, and some of them even got rich from their elocution.

Huge popular acclaim—how cravenly I crave it in my unguarded moments, when the reclusiveness in me unites with the show-off, creating a mutant creature, the Hermit Ham. And so I ask my agent to accept the invitation to . . . wherever. I go to my closet, wondering what to wear.

For Appearance is the other part of this ambivalent experience. When I gave my first reading in that bar I was a winsome twenty-five-year-old in a flippy little skirt (well, that's how I remember her). I am now a woman of a certain age, gray-haired, bespectacled, with a few extra pounds draped around her hips, panting up the midlist hill, sure of never reaching the top no matter what her blurbs maintain. This diagonal journey upwards can be seen as one slant of an X, the X's center being, say, a moment twenty years ago, when I was a blooming fifty-five, gaining literary popularity, losing physical grace. And there at the bottom of *her* diagonal stands a girl looking up hopefully to an imagined elegant celebrity she yearns to become. The inelegant and mildly celebrated author, clutching a podium, drops a glance straight down at the promising young writer below, who has yet to learn, say, that when a verb seems to require an adverb, that verb has revealed its weakness and must be discarded. It may take her a day to find a stronger verb; and more days than anyone can count to invent plots, create imaginary characters and camouflage real ones, settle on a surprising yet inevitable conclusion. As she squints at her still unsatisfactory manuscript she will develop wrinkles, stop working out, forget to replenish her wardrobe even though on the old one safety pins have replaced buttons. This is what it's all about, yells dame to damsel; you will spend most of your working life perfecting your always imperfect prose. You will spend the other part of your working life in front of an audience, reading that prose aloud, wearing bifocals and those safety pins, wondering why you're doing this, hating it, loving it to pieces. Latest in the family that descends from a blind Greek poet through a manic British genius to some fanatic reformers, you will, if you're lucky, feel that your days are well spent. But you may not be lucky, darling. Is your mother still urging you to go to law school? Think about it.

As for me, I suspect that during the twilight of my career I will slide downward on my slant of the X, waving to the valiants on their way up. I will give my final Public Appearance in a bar, refusing the offer of a chair but instead standing on my own two feet, addressing a small crowd of drinkers who'll clap with a show of enthusiasm and then line up so I can autograph their coasters. In my end is my beginning, as the fellow more or less said.

✳
HILDA RAZ

SAY YES

> Body my house,
> my horse, my hound,
> what will I do
> when you are fallen
> MAY SWENSON, "Question"

Frank died in his fifties. Dolly was gone early in her sixties. Jimmy died at forty. Aaron, my grandfather, died when he was sixty. I was six. My nana, Hilda, after whom I am named, died before I was born. That's my family of origin. Father, Mother, Brother, Papa, and Nana. Nobody lived to grow old.

When I was a child, we lived with assorted cousins and aunts in a small house in upstate New York that backed onto the Erie Canal. Railroad tracks ran the length of the canal bed, all the way to New York City. In winter after school we kids would put on our ice skates, climb the hill behind the house, descend to and cross the metal tracks, our skate blades digging into frozen ground between the wooden spacers, to walk gingerly on our serrated toes to Cobb's Hill pond. By the time we got there, the horse-driven Zamboni had cleared the ice right to the far edge of the pond. We'd jump onto the ice, bend double, scissor our legs forward and back, forward and back to skate until darkness fell and then race each other home over the hill, the tracks, and up and down the bank. Then we ate dinner Mother had made. What an idyll. Why did I count the daisies on my bedroom wallpaper every night to fall asleep?

In summer we'd harvest the neighbors' vegetable gardens and forget to weed our own. Not that we even got the produce into the kitchen through the back screened-in porch. We ate standing where we were in the heat, in full sun, our forearms itching like crazy from juice that ran down to our elbows. We stank of chives and raw tomatoes. A secret the neighbors knew. We rode bikes all summer and beyond, until the first snow fell. That's what I remember of my childhood.

Do you believe in denial? My family was Jewish. News of the Holocaust reached our table. My brother Jimmy went off to war when he was sixteen. Our parents signed for him. He left our house for training camp in Virginia during my fourth birthday party. He didn't say good-bye. Who took him to the railroad station?

Later, as an adult writer, I made myself up as a child. A lot happened to that child I made up as she grew up and became an adult writer. For example, at eighteen I became a fiancée when my English professor proposed. Then I became a wife in two ceremonies, one Jewish, one Episcopalian. Then I became a mother when I gave birth, twice. My family of origin was dead, two cancers and two suicides. My new family moved to Nebraska. Then I was a woman who felt as if she had three bodies—her own and her kids'—to continue her line. I was free to continue to invent myself. Nobody knew to say that I walked like Nana, looked like Daddy, spoke like Mother.

Apparently I remained the rebel I'd been. And I published my first book of poems.

Now I needed and wanted a career. Inside the house I continued to write, as I had since childhood, as I worked—in stenographer's notebooks at the kitchen table as I invented dinner, at the swimming pool while minding the children, in the living room while the children watched television, during intermissions in family exchange, and sitting on the kitchen floor in the middle of the night. What was it like, writing my poems? I was born with language in my mouth and few other skills to match it. Therefore my days and some nights were spent reading Swinburne out loud. Now I understand more than the sounds of the words. But the pleasure is the same. Then, as a child and later as a woman, when I picked up my pen, my mouth told my hand what to write. Even now, as my fingers tap the keyboard of my new computer, my mouth waters.

What kept me at it? The ecstasy—now called flow—of writing down words in sequence. No pain in the toe when I kicked that stone, Dr. Johnson. But a real stone for sure. Every experience has language trailing after, language for a writer to catch and wrap up and tie like a bandage. And some experience is made only of language. I became a single parent. The children and I needed money. To jumpstart my career, I said yes to every opportunity. Like Molly Bloom I kept saying yes. For years I taught student poets the only way I could, in borrowed classrooms, until I was a professor and had my own. They let me listen to their language. I read poems with students to help their poems find more language. Or less. Spit out poems.

That's pretty much it. If any advice can be distilled from my long life as a writer and teacher, it's this: say yes.

At thirty years old, and at forty years old, and fifty, and sixty, I found little time to write at home, or even to sit down, except in airplane seats or on trains. I became the editor of *Prairie Schooner*, then a tenured professor, and then a professor with a named chair. The magazine was endowed, I began two book prizes, wrote and published my own books and edited others— and got a lot of necessary help. During my long professional life I was at the head of a literary enterprise with two budgets. Teaching, I joined experienced poets each semester to read new books and wrote our own. I was directing the committees of twelve PhD students at the time I became emerita professor. Many others had graduated with advanced degrees, were teaching, and had published their books. I might have been a thief, or a gambler, or a bad friend, or a pet murderer, without language. Would I trade language for golf skills? No. Only for a brilliant operatic voice. Sometimes. Maybe.

I loved the collaboration of the creative writing classroom. The faculty of the graduate program in poetry included Grace Bauer, Ted Kooser and me. Many of our students came to us with MFAs, teaching experience, and publications—some books and chapbooks—in print. They were eager to write new work. We sat at an oval table, twelve students and teacher, to discuss and often write the beginnings of poems that became the nexus of our first or next books. And because many poets passed through our classrooms, we witnessed and participated in the process of creation. This teaching became the anchor of my professional life. The delight of witness, which often I called voyeurism, never faltered over decades—the same delight that Robert Lowell's seminar at Boston University provided us students when he read the new poems that became *Life Studies*, a book that changed the nature of contemporary poetry.

"Caring for myself is not self-indulgence, it is self-preservation, and that is an act of political warfare." This quote from poet Audre Lorde became my manifesto. I joined Lorde, and others, by caring for myself as an act of political warfare. Women like me seemed not to be welcome in the halls of academe or anywhere else outside the house except in specific gender-identified roles—as a secretary or an assistant, for example—when I began my career. Nevertheless I cared for myself through the start and development of my life as a poet—and also through illness, breast cancer, by writing two books, and by editing a special issue of a magazine titled *Disruptions: the body, the family, cultures, genders, the state, and the world*. Through two divorces and a third marriage I took care of myself, the kids, and the magazine, the book series, spouses, friends, households, and students by running around a lot, reading, teaching, and writing more books. It was a good and exhausting life.

I was seventy-two years old when the chair of the department of English told me the correct word was "tweet," not "twittering," and I decided *not* to blog, learn website design, or distribute journals on digital devices. I hired a digital media specialist to manage web production. Our graduate students were publishing well and getting jobs. In the fall, a new generation of students came into the office and sat down to ask about success, not art. I found a good therapist.

The therapist poured out two glasses of water and asked in a chilly voice, "Do you want to die at your desk?" She said she was just asking. My mentor, the Cather and Keats scholar Bernice Slote, had died at her desk, which was now my desk. Well, she'd had her final stroke there. Her successor Hugh Luke had stayed at that desk through his final illness. It seemed to be a *PS* tradition. In truth, I *had* thought to die at my desk or in the classroom. But the distance between now and death seemed tedious—new details to work out, new clothes to buy and wear. I went home and resigned from my job.

We put a *For Sale* sign in front of the house where we'd lived for thirty years. We stored our belongings in PODS and lived in an empty house, with a borrowed bed, a card table, and four chairs. Soon our house had new owners, two women and their teenaged daughter; they carried in carton after carton of the same books we'd carried out. We returned the bed, table, and chairs, packed the car, and left the city where we'd lived through our adult lives.

Our new house sits on the lip of an arroyo, an hour by rail to Santa Fe, twenty minutes by car to Albuquerque. We have four sliding doors that lead outside. The high desert is different from upstate New York where I grew up among many things green, my tall brother studying, writing equations, going off to war, my red-bearded Papa on the back stoop, cleaning the fish he'd caught, my mother and father whispering in the kitchen. It is different from the Middle West where flat land meets the curve of the horizon, where I worked as a professor, my brilliant students writing books that others would teach, my beloved children setting off firecrackers in the driveway, lying in the warm storm drain reading, coming in only to empty the refrigerator I'd filled. The high desert is beige and sunlit in the shadow of mountains, beautiful.

And here, surprisingly, as always has been, I am not at home. Not here or anywhere. Not at home when I open one of the four doors, and walk the arroyo each afternoon at 4:00. Not when I sit at my new desk reading manuscripts or writing. Not when the early light makes me want to be a painter, or an opera singer, and we get up for coffee and walk the long gravel road to bend down for the newspaper. Not when I stand at the sink to rub the charred skin off Big Jim peppers, or plop a straw hat on my head, or reach for the big sunglasses and the Nalgene water bottle. Not when the coyotes call through the open window two feet away from our heads on the pillows. Not when the heat sends me to read under the ceiling fan.

Would you say that I am old? Living here feels like the pause between thought and action. Between finding the subject and making the poem. Living here is the long breath, the attenuated beat in a syncopated chord or the pause before the line turns.

How does age inform my current work? I'm calmer and can sit longer. I have a sore thumb so the space bar is a challenge. I have more time and can go to the desk more often. I know the aura that signals a necessary phrase or sentence, even a word. *Haboob*, a wall of dust.

I don't know how to grow older except to breathe. Nobody taught me. My family didn't have time to grow old. I didn't have time to learn to garden either, only to pick produce other people had planted. (A good definition of an editor, right?) Sitting on a chaise, even to read May Sarton's journal at seventy, is not a familiar posture. My sore knees stick out and I'm restless. Not being at home wherever I am is my familiar state and condition. I don't mind. The idyll of childhood is only one story. Death is coming for sure. The story of becoming old is not a story I know or want to tell. Ambiguity is the life of art. My friend from high school, long gone from my life, suddenly reappeared as a New Mexico neighbor. She asks me, "As a poet, are you writing from a place of aging? Or from the place of all you've experienced, witnessed, lost, discovered, understood, not understood? Doesn't this mean that being over sixty or seventy is almost irrelevant?" What good questions.

In choosing to move, I'd expected to continue to find answers. To begin, I learned everything necessary for my new life: a laptop computer is easier to use than one riveted to the desk. A smart phone can be answered anywhere. My forty-year-old habit of saying yes is useful: I have a new job as director of the endowed poetry series for the University of New Mexico Press, and another as poetry editor for a small magazine, *Bosque*. I'm still teaching. What's the difference between my old life and this one? Less work, less travel, less worry, less responsibility, more time to dream at my desk, write poems, and watch the bobcat saunter across the arroyo. Someone else works at the endowment for the poetry series I direct. The budget isn't mine. I'm no longer CEO of a literary enterprise but a worker in a field I know and love. Do I say no? Not yet.

I'd wanted to continue to invent answers, to invent old age just as I'd invented solutions to work, the flood in the basement, and even myself as a successful writer in the work force. We moved to the mountains of New Mexico ready to try to find a new geography. Can I *solve* growing old? Nobody I know has gone before me into old age. Is the distance between life and death infinite? Maybe. I think so. Each part divides before us as we go. The days, thanks to brain chemistry, fly before me as I go. The mountain over our house seems eternal.

So many different stories to tell, the products of our pasts.

My past is over. I've occupied the traditional roles. I've had a profession and a career. I've fought the establishment for gender and social equity alongside many brave women and men. My stories now will have to do with where I am, still a stranger at my desk. They are all the sum of all my life. Soon I will be older. Everything familiar is past. That joy informs each day and night, each moment at the sink as my thumbs roll char off the peppers.

We get up early to walk the long road to the mailbox and walk back to the house to drink coffee. Later in the day it's wine or beer, wine or lemonade. And always water, lots of water. I smear a kind of new cream over my damp body after the shower, a brief shower in the desert where the well gives sweet water, for now. Our house is nice, big rooms, high windows, light, light, light. My new study where I write has the same dimensions as my old study where I wrote. Yesterday I bought a good pair of hiking boots, my first, to wear while exploring the mountains, with the help of my friend from high school, who is a writer and a naturalist. She and I smile at each other over coffee. How did we get here? In a flash I remember her pirouetting on the diagonal across the floor in the dance classroom where we met, in Rochester, New York. We wear the same blue leotards and tights. We are not yet thirteen. She is exactly the same as she was. In the flash, and after, I am exactly the same as I was. Our friendship is the same friendship. She is, as she was, a much better dancer than I am.

The world in the high desert blooms through the drought. Jackrabbits the size of dogs run in the arroyos. In the bushes at the head of the road, a rattlesnake appears and disappears. A red house finch sits on the feeder and trills. From across the fields, an answer. A brown tarantula the size of my father's palm crawls over the gravel pile toward our porch. "See this hand?" he glowers, bending over to show me.

The economy falters, the world is changing. Civilizations rise and fall and rise again. Pain and atrocity prevail. What else is new under the sun? Poetry itself survives. The poems of Yeats and Whitman survive, and those of Lorde, and Plath and Sexton. Muriel Rukeyser and Stanley Kunitz and Maxine Kumin teach me not how to grow old but how to write about it. Scholars and editors are busy finding new work by old writers. Maybe I'll invent an old female body for myself, one that wears hiking boots, finds and makes friends, and enters each day with fear and delight, her hands reaching for the keyboard.

✳
JANE SMILEY

BOYS AND GIRLS

A couple of months ago, my farrier, a lifelong horseman about
my age, asked me if I remembered a song by Judy Collins about
someone who rode in a rodeo. Did I ever! Early in the winter
of 1968, I introduced myself to a Yale basketball player who
happened to be from Wyoming, my first westerner. I developed a serious crush, and I accompanied and cultivated that
crush with repeated doses of "Someday Soon," a song by Ian
Tyson that Judy Collins recorded on her album *Who Knows
Where the Time Goes?* My crush had never been on a horse,
but he was always traveling with the basketball team (that year
to Hawaii), his family had a cabin in the Big Horn Mountains,
that was enough for me.

I laughed at myself and promised to make a CD of the Judy
Collins album and give it to my farrier. What happened when
I put my copy on my own player after downloading it was that
I burst into tears. *Who Knows Where the Time Goes?* came
out in November 1968, my sophomore year at Vassar. I had a
room to myself that year—I can still picture the desk by the

windows, which looked out onto the grass and the walk in front of my dorm. My stereo was engineered to fold up into a suitcase-like portable object. It sat on my trunk in front of the closet, and like all stereos of the day, you could set it to play a series of records or to play the same record over and over. I would have bought Judy Collins's album at once, because I already had *In My Life* and *Wildflowers*. It was a truism of the day that you had to listen to a record multiple times in order to appreciate it, and so I did. Judy had a crystal clear voice and she sang, among others, "The Story of Isaac," by Leonard Cohen, her own "My Father," Bob Dylan's "I Pity the Poor Immigrant," Sandy Denny's "Who Knows Where the Time Goes," another Leonard Cohen, "Bird on the Wire," and "Pretty Polly," a traditional ballad in the voice of a young man luring a girl he has promised to marry away to her murder. All of these songs were melodious, but I see now that Collins's great virtue was that she sang the words clearly, and the words, for me, were strange and fascinating, not like anything I was familiar with back home in middle-class suburban St. Louis, Missouri.

Other than "Someday Soon," the one I listened to most was "The Story of Isaac." I was not reared in a religious household, so I knew nothing about Abraham setting out to sacrifice his son. Cohen's details were riveting: "So we started up the mountain / I was running, he was walking / And his axe was made of gold." So was the admonition, "When it all comes down to dust / I will kill you if I must, / I will love you if I can. / Collins' voice was pure and cold. I could picture the child, I could picture the father, I felt that she meant what she said. "Bird on the Wire" was more enigmatic, and also in a lower key—more regretful. "And if I, if I have been untrue, / I

hope you know, that it was not to you." I had never been untrue to anyone—I was still aspiring to that opportunity. Collins made it sound complex, inevitable, and worth thinking
about. As for "I Pity the Poor Immigrant," I listened to that
one a thousand times without knowing what Bob Dylan and
Judy Collins were talking about, but the words themselves,
the paradoxes of Dylan's argument, kept me listening. If "I
Pity the Poor Immigrant" had been a poem in a textbook,
I might have read it twice; I would not have memorized it,
but since it was a song, I did memorize it, along with all the
others, and not intentionally.

Over the last twenty years, I have been repeatedly asked
where my aesthetic came from, my desire to write, my sense
of what literature was, and I have always given the same answer—after *Oliver Twist*, I gradually made my way to three
books, *David Copperfield*, *Giants in the Earth*, and *The Web of
Life*, all assigned in the ninth grade. Suddenly, my understanding woke up. I not only comprehended David's world, full
of rich characters and lush language, I enjoyed it; I not only
could picture the flat, cruel Dakota prairie, I could empathize
with those who found themselves there. And my little biology
textbook about ecology drew the big picture for me, showing
me how everything was necessarily interconnected, a system
rather than a picture. But another thing happened in ninth
grade, too, and I now realize how deeply that event shaped
me—I was given a portable phonograph for Christmas. I set
it up in my room, and I spent hours and hours, day and night,
listening to LP records. Every day, year after year for eight
years, that phonograph and its successor poured words into
my brain. I thought I was listening to music, but what I was
taking in was far more, and I now think that my aesthetic and

my worldview owe much more than I ever realized not only to Judy Collins, but to Joni Mitchell, Bob Dylan, Leonard Cohen, Joan Baez, and Sandy Denny.

The Dylan song I loved best was on Peter, Paul, and Mary's 1967 release, *Album 1700*, "Bob Dylan's Dream." I had been a Peter, Paul, and Mary fan from the earliest days of my phonograph. We sang "If I Had a Hammer" (Pete Seeger) around the campfire at summer camp, and "Where Have All the Flowers Gone?" (also Pete Seeger) gave me the same creeps as the postapocalyptic novel *On the Beach*. We also sang "Blowin' in the Wind," which I then heard on Peter, Paul, and Mary's 1963 album, *In the Wind*. But "Bob Dylan's Dream" wasn't about politics, it was about friendship and nostalgia, which as a freshman in college, I was just old enough to begin to appreciate. Dylan wasn't much older than I was—eight years—and yet could write, "I wish, I wish, I wish in vain that we could sit simply in that room once again." Listening to his "Dream," it was as though I was experiencing my own life in the present and the future simultaneously. Possibly for the first time, I sensed the fleeting nature of existence.

The great female exponent of Dylan's music in those days was Joan Baez. I played her two-disc recording of Dylan songs, *Any Day Now*, over and over. It came out a month after "Who Knows Where the Time Goes?" I dimly knew that Baez and Dylan had a friendship of some kind, and that they lived in California, but I didn't read gossip magazines or *Rolling Stone*, so I had no stories to back up the songs. I was also used to my cultural icons (Charles Dickens, Laura Lee Hope) being dead or anonymous. I would lie in the darkness, staring at the moonlight on the ceiling of my room, and let the words do the storytelling. They only partly made sense. I loved the tune of "Sad-Eyed Lady of the Lowlands," but I had no idea what "sheets like metal" meant, or why her deck of cards would be "missing the jack and the ace." Did he love her? Did he dislike her? Was "she" Joan Baez, so that he was writing about her and she was singing about herself? What were her "matchbook songs" or her "gypsy hymns"? But when Baez's voice deepened into the refrain, "Sad-eyed lady of the lowlands, where the sad-eyed prophets say that no man comes . . ." I gave up parsing it out and was carried along once again. The song ran almost twelve minutes—lulling me to sleep, entering my dreams.

But my favorite song on *Any Day Now* was "Restless Farewell." "Restless Farewell" is Dylan's apologia for sins he may have committed. Supposedly, it is based on an Irish tune, "The Parting Glass," but the lyrics differ considerably, and they seemed very current to me in 1969—"Oh, every foe that ever I've faced, / the cause was there before we came. /And every cause that ever I fought, / I fought it full, without regret or shame." I imagined the cause to be political, maybe the Vietnam War, and I admired the idea that there could be a full commitment, but also a change of heart. However, I think the verse that struck me most was the farewell to past romances. After saying that she meant no harm in the relationships she has had, she says: "to remain as friends, you need the time, / to make amends and stay behind, /and since my feet are now fast, and point away from the past, / I'll bid farewell and be down the line." I, of course, was only just beginning with the first person I might ever bid farewell to, so this verse did not reflect my feelings or my experience, but it did tell me, maybe for the first time, that a girl, a woman, could have a series of relationships and then bid farewell and be down the line. No novelist ever suggested this. If a girl did not end up like Elizabeth Bennet, married happily to Mr. Darcy, then she would end up like Dorothea Brooke, making a single serious mistake (though fortunately with an older man who would likely die soon) before finding a suitable peer.

Reinforcing "Restless Farewell" on *Any Day Now* was "One Too Many Mornings," in which the young woman wakes up to the recognition that she needs to get moving. "It's a restless hungry feelin' that don't mean no one no good / When everything I'm sayin' you can say it just as good. / You were right from your side, but I was right from mine. / We're both just one too many mornings, and a thousand miles behind." The androgynous nature of love, romance, and sexuality is implicit in these covers of Dylan songs by women singers with beautiful soprano voices who made sure, if need be, to speak in a tough-guy patois. His message was her message was his message.

I learned the same lesson from Tom Rush and Joni Mitchell, both of whom sang Mitchell's song, "Urge for Going." I was already a fan of Tom Rush before "The Circle Game" came out, also in November 1968. He sang, "I had a girl in summertime, / with summer-colored skin. / And not another man in town, my darlin's heart could win. / And when the leaves fell tremblin' down, / and bully winds did rub their faces in the snow, / she got the urge for goin', / and I had to let her go." She goes, he can't seem to do anything about it, nor can he seem to make up his own mind to leave. Six months later, when Mitchell put out her version of the song, on *Clouds*, the sexes were reversed—he was the one to leave; she was the one to pull the blankets to her chin in despair.

My favorite Tom Rush song, and one of my favorite songs of all time, was "No Regrets," which reinforces the sense of the man being passively abandoned by the woman—"No regrets. No tears good-bye. / Don't wantcha back / we'd only cry again / Say good-bye again." Rush also covered a Tom Paxton song I knew from high school, "The Last Thing on my Mind": "Are you goin' away with no word of farewell? Will there be not a trace left behind?" In these songs, relationships come and go, the girls have agency, both sexes are equally fluid, and both sexes have similar feelings. These singers were my peers— rather like older brothers and sisters. I paid attention to their experience.

Joni Mitchell's album, *Clouds*, came out in May 1969. Mitchell possessed her own music, but Collins and Baez possessed theirs too—the singer's voice asserts possession of the sentiments expressed and the words that express them. Even so, Mitchell existed in my consciousness beside Dylan, Cohen, Rush, and Paxton, her voice, her music, her lyrics flowing out of my stereo and into my brain, usually at night, usually when I was alone, usually when I was doing nothing else but listening to the music. My crush had become my boyfriend, and of course our relationship was complex—the song "Both Sides Now" reassured me—"Tears and fears and feeling proud / To say 'I love you' right out loud . . . / I've looked at life from both sides now, / from up and down, and still somehow, / it's life's illusions I recall, / I really don't know life at all." Maybe the song I listened to most on *Clouds* was "That Song about the Midway," in which Mitchell recounts her attraction to what my mother would have considered a very suspect character: "You were betting on some lover, you were shaking up the dice, / and I thought I saw you cheating once or twice." The song recognizes that unsavory characters can be quite alluring—"You were playing like a devil wearing wings." But as the song progresses, Mitchell comes to identify with the man, not desire him—he has preceded her down the midway, and now she wonders how she, too, might escape the exhausting chaos she finds herself in.

One great virtue of Mitchell's music for an aspiring writer is how pictorial her lyrics are. This is evident in "Tin Angel," in which Mitchell catalogues knickknacks around her house, "varnished weeds in window jars," then decides to throw out these markers of former times because, "I found someone to love today." She knows perfectly well that he is an iffy proposition—a tin angel—"What will happen if I try / To place another heart in him?" The austerity of the tune and of her performance implies that these hopes aren't justified, that her ambivalence is real.

The late sixties and early seventies were, I think, a unique time to be in college. There were plenty of girls in my dorm who were Vassar girls with traditional aspirations—find a promising youth from a good family and get married—but they were no longer the norm. My roommate wanted to be a playwright, I wanted to be a novelist, a girl down the hall wanted to be a doctor, as did one of the girls who had a car and drove me to my weekends at Yale. One girl planned to be an accountant, another a physicist, another to go into publishing. The girl behind me in line at orientation turned out to be Meryl Streep—she never told me her ambitions, but they quickly became evident. The boys I knew were less definite, I think in part because they were middle-class kids disoriented at finding themselves at Yale, in the bastion of privilege and luxury. And the draft was hanging over them, sapping their attention, sapping their ambition. It was not only that we girls wanted to do things, it was also that there now were places to

be filled—slots in law schools and medical schools and graduate schools. I don't remember any of us discussing how hard
it would be to attain our goals, or talking about the forces ar-
rayed against us, much less any inherent mental or intellectual
deficits we might have that would prevent us. Much later, I
talked about this with a friend who was born in 1941 and graduated from UC Berkeley in 1962. She and her boyfriend (later
her husband) acted in student productions, and apparently
they were a sensation—beautiful, talented, charismatic—but
all anyone said was that they should get married, never that
she should strike out on her own and make her own career.
Such a thing wasn't thought of, she told me.

Another song I listened to over and over in 1969 was "Percy's
Song," by Bob Dylan, sung by Sandy Denny and the Fairport
Convention. Perhaps the words that first struck me were "Joliet
prison." It wasn't often that a place I was familiar with turned
up in a song—but over the years, traveling back and forth to
Chicago to visit my cousins, we had passed near Joliet, Illinois,
several times. The story in the song is clear—after a fatal accident, the intoxicated young driver of one of the vehicles is sent
to prison for ninety-nine years. The singer of the song goes
to the judge to plead for clemency, and the judge is adamant,
"The judge he spoke out of the side of his mouth, . . . saying
the witness who saw, he left with no doubt . . . too late, too
late, for his case it is sealed, his sentence is passed, and cannot be repealed . . . At that the judge jumped forward, and his
face it did freeze, sayin' 'Could you kindly leave my office now,
please.'" A few moments later, Denny sings, "I walked down
the courthouse stairs and did not understand." Of course, now,
forty years later, I do understand—driving under the influence

is a serious crime; there are sentencing guidelines, procedures must be followed, a clemency plea from a random young person is a waste of time—but when I was twenty, I did not understand the excuses for what seemed to be evident injustice. Dylan's song was not about the Vietnam War and my friends being drafted, but it might as well have been—it perfectly encapsulated our only possible response to an incomprehensible system: art.

And one of my favorite songs (I would sit by the phonograph, moving the arm so that it would replay the cut again and again) was "White Rabbit," in which Grace Slick, whose voice was absolutely authoritative, told me about an alternate reality that was available to me at any time. Her vibrato was compelling, her forte building to her fortissimo was electrifying, and the words, which she had written, were more riveting and knowledgeable than any other song on the album, the lyrics of which often subsided into, "Well, you know what I mean."

I wrote my first novel between September 1970 and May 1971—it made use of the materials at hand, and was about students not unlike myself, negotiating the mysteries of relationships, trying to find passion but also safety in spite of their minimal understanding of each other and of themselves. It seemed dramatic at the time. My teacher gave me an A. Since then, I've often demeaned it, never reread it. But what I got from it was important—confidence, familiarity, discipline. I learned how to use the tools, and that the tools were worth using. I never had a doubt that it was my opening shot, not my last chance. As the next few years passed, I learned something else from my musical mentors—they had plenty more to say. Judy Collins, Joni Mitchell, Joan Baez, Leonard Cohen, and Bob Dylan came out with more records, most of which I faithfully bought and listened to again and again. They accompanied me across country, into and out of relationships, into and out of ideas. I learned from them that there was no distinction between the feelings of boys and the feelings of girls, between the thoughts of boys and the thoughts of girls, between the words of boys and the words of girls. Because I listened to them in the privacy of my room, without seeing them on stage, I did not have to picture what the girls were wearing, how they were presenting themselves, who was the boss. Every singer of every song had complete authority while singing that song. Girls and boys were equally free—that is what I learned. When I was writing my novel, I had not one single thought about whether a girl could or should be doing this, whether a girl had fewer rights or a more limited consciousness than a boy.

The music scene evolved, of course. Rock and roll went back to being masculine, as it had been when I first fell for the Beatles. Girls, with a few exceptions like Deborah Harry, were consigned to the audience again. In 1979, when my eighteen-month-old daughter was learning to dance around the living room, Blondie's biggest song, "Heart of Glass," was presented much differently from, say, "Suzanne," a Leonard Cohen song on Judy Collins's album, *In My Life*. Harry's voice, singing the lyrics, disappeared into the fabric of the orchestration, hard to hear and relatively meaningless.

Listening to those albums in college, I thought that I loved the haunting tunes, but they were the gateway drug, you might say. That what I was memorizing turned out to be some of the great lyric poetry of the latter half of the twentieth century was not something I thought about, that the words that were pouring into my brain were idiosyncratic and challenging was not something I recognized, but now, when I listen to "The Story of Isaac," "My Father," "Restless Farewell," or "That Song about the Midway," I thank those artists for that most of all.

*

LAURA TOHE

THE STORIES FROM WHICH I COME

My little community on the rez harbored no writers, no television, no fluoridated water. No newspapers landed at our door. On one wall sat a shelf of encyclopedias that my mother had paid for in careful installments from her small budget. My brothers and I were to handle the books carefully and put them away when finished with them. I rarely read them or used them for my homework. My imagination yearned to fly beyond the pages of *Birds of North America* and the list of US presidents. I wanted more than facts and figures. I wanted to read stories about lives beyond my little community of Crystal—where we were sometimes snowed in for days in the heart of winter—beyond the trading post, four churches, the elementary school with one bus, one army jeep, and the dirt road that led north and south. My escape was through the radio, comic books, romance magazines, and the library books we checked out from the Gallup Public Library more than eighty miles away. I didn't *see* until much later how my mother's and my relatives' stories had always surrounded my life.

When darkness settled in, the radio waves carried the only rock 'n' roll station from Oklahoma City into our living room, which is how my brothers and I kept up with the latest hits. My mother didn't graduate from high school, but she saw to it that we did our homework and she watched our grades. Probably that is why my mother took us to the library. I checked out fairy-tale books with literary roots in Russia and Europe—a girl whose heart was so pure that gold fell on her when she walked through a doorway fascinated me. And the witch who lived in a house that stood on chicken legs added more fodder for my imagination. Through books and stories I could travel all over the world. Through the library's time machine I could eavesdrop on the people making stories in times past. In contrast to these colorful stories, in school I learned to read from the Dick and Jane series that was a monotony of repetition. "Oh see Sally jump. Oh, Oh, Oh." I learned the alphabet quickly and how letters are put together to form words, sentences, and stories. Once I caught on, I mostly taught myself how to read. I finished the book. The teacher had me tutor my classmates in reading.

All my classmates were Diné and barely spoke English, if at all. At home both of my parents spoke Diné bizaad/Navajo language and English, so I entered school being bilingual. We were living in the era of boarding schools and assimilation, the time when Indigenous identity and language were at risk. To speak our native language in school was stepping into precarious space, because we were punished for it. I tutored my classmates and saved them from punishment for speaking our language, lest they stand in the corner or in the hallway, or get their hands slapped with a ruler. Ironically, my father had been a Navajo code talker during WWII as part of a select group of Navajo marines who devised a secret code in the Navajo language that they used to successfully transmit messages over the radio waves while in combat in the South Pacific islands. The Japanese cryptographers could not decipher this unbreakable code. It was quick, accurate, and helped save countless American lives. My parents' generation came to believe that to learn to speak English, to read and write the white man's language, was a way to become "successful" in that world. Sadly, this was often at the expense of losing our native languages. I bring this up as context for my development as a writer.

In the early 1960s I didn't read Indigenous writers; I didn't know that any existed. Every day at reading time, out came the further monotony of Dick, Jane, Sally, and Spot. In fourth grade, the teacher introduced storytelling in the classroom. From memory he told us "The Tell-Tale Heart," "The Raven," and other stories that formed my love for Edgar Allan Poe's work. Two years later my teacher read Laura Ingalls Wilder to us every day after lunch. Hearing and reading stories in English regularly, I thought only non-Indians were writers or could be, even though when I was twelve, I secretly longed to be a writer. As my mother drove us down the dusty rez road, I thought of how I could become a writer. What stories could I tell? Who would be interested in my stories? How does one become a writer? Instead I told my parents I wanted to be a pediatrician when I grew up.

I didn't realize until much later that my writing life really began with my mother's stories and the stories my relatives told as I was growing up. Not until I graduated from university with a degree in psychology did I stop writing "in secret." Fear and my lack of confidence stifled me from putting words

on paper. I was growing up when President Kennedy was as-
sassinated and during President Johnson's war on poverty, so
I thought I could make a difference if I worked in the mental
health field for my community. Though I didn't pursue a graduate degree in psychology, I think studying it as an undergraduate helped me understand something of human behavior. On
our shopping trips "to town" Mom sometimes told my brothers and me stories that her great-grandmother told her. Most
vivid is the one about a brother and sister who transformed
into prairie dogs due to their parents' neglect; it was the first
story I wrote and published. My instructor and mentor told
me I had a wealth of stories from my community and that I
might write about that. I came to an epiphany—stories and
storytellers had surrounded me all my life and I could write
those stories.

Storytelling was and still is a large part of my social interaction. My relatives' stories ranged from the mundane to
the supernatural. Stories were tidbits, advisory, cautionary,
historic, and horrific. On my visits home from the Midwest—
where I lived for over a decade—Grandma, Uncle, and I sat
at the kitchen table over breakfast, while Grandma filled me
in on all the goings-on while I was away. Uncle added details
where Grandma forgot. She was the Navajo version of the
National Enquirer. By the time the dishes were put aside and
we were drinking the last of the coffee, I learned about who
had had a "lost weekend," about what happened to the sheep-
herder, about a woman who had two husbands, about a rela-
tive who had a car accident and was in the hospital recuperat-
ing. One story led into another story. They were always told in
a mixture of Navajo and English, and even though some were
sad, there was always the laughter. Such storytelling sessions

brought us together after we'd been separated by time and distance. Sometimes Grandma told of where our ancestors originated and how they came to settle in Lupton, Arizona. It seemed almost everyone in my family was a storyteller. My father told a story of how the power lines were placed not far from his hogan by a helicopter hovering above, and another of how he kept the coyotes from killing the sheep. My mother always said, "Without stories one is an empty person." I used to tuck little stories away for her on my drive home—until I would suddenly remember that she had passed on.

Most of my elder relatives are gone now, and I miss our storytelling sessions over the kitchen table. There is a younger generation who continue the tradition, like my niece, who, when she comes to visit me in the city, brings the news from the rez about our family and any scandals taking place on the rez. The stories are similar to Grandma's stories, but the names have changed. The roots of my writing began with the oral tradition; it formed the foundation of my writing life.

One might think that with the Internet and e-books the oral tradition has eroded. Instead, storytelling continues but in a different format. Social sites like Facebook encourage the continuation of stories among a large group of friends and family, albeit among those who have access to the Internet. We keep up with each other's news—my pinon-picking trip, a friend's first day of teaching, the passing of a family member, another friend's spiritual walk to save the San Francisco Peaks. The stories daily flood Facebook.

I am no longer as hard-pressed to find Indigenous poets, novelists, journalists, and essayists publishing their work as I was when I was growing up with only the Dick and Jane reading series. A renaissance of literature by Indigenous writers is happening all over North and South America. It began with writers such as Leslie Marmon Silko, Scott Momaday, Simon Ortiz, and James Welch. A younger generation of Indigenous American voices is creating new literary styles and winning prestigious national awards. These writers have even moved out of the anthropology and Indian Studies section of the surviving bookstores to the American Literature section. The classic oral tradition still influences my creative work as when I wrote *Enemy Slayer: A Navajo Oratorio,* a commissioned piece for the Phoenix Symphony Orchestra. The timing for this libretto grew out of the Middle-Eastern war and merges poetry with chorus and classical music and broke new ground for my work and for the space where it was performed.

As an "older writer" I see the tremendous social, political, and literary changes that have occurred in this country, many of which I once felt as alienation. I grew up in the era of the civil rights movement, Vietnam, the feminist movement, the American Indian movement, and the rock 'n' roll music that often accompanied the questioning of America's history. These tremendous political and social transformations continue to inform my work and form the context out of which I write. Writing enables me to have a voice, to claim my place in my continued development as poet, storyteller, and librettist. I didn't get here alone; I have a long chain of storytellers behind me, those who knew that having stories is not to be an empty person. Learning to speak, read, and write the white man's language has brought me "success" in terms of the works I've published and invitations to travel to read my work locally and internationally.

A few years go I attended Diné College, the first community college founded by my tribal nation, to become literate in my native language. The years of literary assimilation are now behind me, and I sometimes write and publish in the Navajo language. I recently published an oral history book in Navajo and English of the Navajo code talkers. The younger generation of Diné people will have another text to read in the Navajo language, and in this way my work contributes to a cultural maintenance of language and oral tradition. The stories from which I come are part of a journey that began centuries ago with the oral tradition and are now part of the written tradition; a journey filled with love for language, sounds, and images.

HILMA WOLITZER

WHAT I KNOW

One of the perks of the writing profession—if you don't go on television to plug your book or plaster your photo on the back cover—is that nobody really has to know how old you are or what you look like. Your wardrobe doesn't matter, either. You never even have to change out of the pajamas in which you may work, as I do, going directly from bed to desk each morning (or, as Amy Tan puts it, "from dream to dream"). Sometimes, lost in a fictional universe, as a writer or a reader, I'll be surprised by my reflection on the way to the kitchen or the bathroom. So *that's* who I've become! Yet an author's age is often mentioned, if not stressed, in reviews and discussions of books, especially those written by women "of a certain age," that coy euphemism for old.

I've always been aware of the limits and advantages of a writer's particular age. At seven or eight, I sat under the kitchen table, eavesdropping on the grownups and storing that thrilling stuff—the coming attractions of life—like a squirrel gathering acorns for winter. That is, until someone noticed me and they all quickly lapsed into Yiddish or Pig Latin—"*Ixnay, the idkay!*" Still, there was my own experience to mine. Flannery O'Connor once famously said, "Anybody who has survived his childhood has enough information about life to last him the rest of his days." I believe she was referring to writers and their material. But all I wrote back then was the usual juvenilia about the seasons, as if I'd invented them: "Spring has come all over again / Out of the houses come women and men / Young and old with a joyous cheer / Did not you know that spring is here?" I have no idea where that odd locution came from—no one I knew in Brooklyn sounded like that.

At twelve, advised by an English teacher to write about what I knew, but already prevaricating (like a true preadolescent), I penned verse about being blind, or a refugee, or an unwed mother. In my twenties and thirties, mired in domesticity, I wrote domestic stories in which Jell-O appeared almost as frequently as it did at my dinner table. The first of those stories to be published was called "Today a Woman Went Mad in the Supermarket." Taking that English teacher's advice, at last! And with a first novel in print at forty-four, I was sometimes billed as the "Great Middle-Aged Hope."

Now, in my eighties, and with a photo to prove it on the back of my latest book, age has become both a positive and negative factor in my career. Isn't that great—she's still working! But who wants to read something written by somebody's grandmother? As science extends longevity—there will soon be more of us than of them—society remains stubbornly ageist, ravenous for the newest, youngest best thing. And although we're gaining on them in numbers, those kids keep coming up like chorus girls, in all the arts.

Actress Estelle Parsons, who first appeared on stage when

she was six years old and is still going strong almost eight decades later, doesn't feel displaced by younger actors because
she's "still able to inhabit characters from sixteen to one hundred and five." Novelists, of course, have similar freedom. We
can all be ingénues or ancients in our minds and on the page.

The painter Gerald Monroe isn't fazed by the culture of
youth, either. In his own youth, he says, he had "unrealistic"
fantasies about fame and fortune, about galleries, collectors,
and reviews. At eighty-six, he's unencumbered by that consuming ambition. The work is what draws him to his studio,
and his ongoing sense of himself as an engaged, functioning
artist, whose influences are now interior. Process, for him,
from that first mark on the blank canvas, is everything.

That brings me to the blank page, where a first mark must
also be made. But what does one write about late in life? The
prolific Philip Roth, nearly eighty now, an age when people
are more likely to exchange biopsy results than reports of sexual conquests, has expressed surprise that illness isn't a more
popular subject for fiction than adultery. They both still seem
like viable and nonexclusive themes to me, but a new self-
consciousness has set in with my dotage. Shall I look backward or forward? Inward or outward? Who is my audience
now? And what do I really know, anyway, after all those years
of experience? If I'd only realized I was going to commit myself
to this occupation, I might have lived a more interesting life.

All that fretful consideration can stymie the creative impulse or even take the place of writing itself. It probably contributed to the twelve-year block I suffered in that (relatively
youthful) period between my early sixties and midseventies. It
was a terribly restless time, when my very identity seemed at
stake. A writer is someone who writes, which I agonized about

daily without effect. I had chronic insomnia in bed, but would fall asleep immediately at the computer. If anyone asked what I was working on, as my more productive friends were given to do, I'd try to appear suitably discreet rather than stricken.

I'm not exactly sure how what threatened to become a terminal block was finally resolved. Several of those fallow years tripped miserably by until, reluctantly and without much hope, I entered psychotherapy in search of a cause and a cure. After a stretch of pondering the possibilities of inhibition, depression, lowered energy, or simply having lost my writing ability—without coming to an absolute conclusion—I began to write a novel about a woman with a mysterious psychic ache who goes into therapy to figure it out. She and I were both saved by the strategy (although a two-book contract was another incentive for me).

The other day a friend lamented that she can no longer write the way she did when she was young. I think I know what she means. That wonderfully optimistic ebullience has vanished. You don't just start scribbling with the confidence that something good will come of it, no matter how lousy it seems at first. Time is sharply finite, and language isn't at your fingertips anymore. I lose about a noun a day lately. Words fall off and roll out of sight like loose buttons. I confess to needing my thesaurus more than ever, and to reading other writers in order to replenish my vocabulary as well as for the usual pleasures.

Another friend told me that her mother, an indefatigable knitter, began a new project as soon as she finished a previous one. Her family decided that her nonstop knitting was a superstitious hedge against death, which would never dare claim her while she was making a sweater for one of her grandchildren, who might be left with a one-sleeved pullover. Is that why I want so much to continue working—not just because it's what I *do*, but because it might have some magical sway over my mortality? Or, maybe, as aging claims faculties like vision and hearing and memory and mobility, the world of the imagination becomes an escape and a solace.

I honestly don't know. Perhaps I just keep doing it to feed my ego. There have been so many rewards over the years: the joys of friendship with other writers; letters from readers who'd felt the shock of recognition in my novels; the ability to earn a living (of sorts) from writing; and teaching gigs to make up the difference. Best of all, there's the intense gratification of the work itself.

Praise and encouragement have been gratifying, too. Even when I was a child—the middle daughter of three and probably craving attention—my nonliterary parents saw some value in those awful early poems. They invited me to recite them during breaks in their weekly gin rummy game. The card players always clapped politely before dealing out the next hand, and the shuffling cards were like an echo of their applause. Then, during open-school week, my third-grade teacher, Miss Fredericks, told my mother that I showed "great promise," news that she carried home with pride to my father and me. Later, I was voted poet laureate of my junior high school. And much later there was a spate of published books—novels for adults and for children that received prominent positive reviews. It was all pretty heady.

But of course there were also negative reviews—against which there is no defense, in the world or within oneself—and remaindered, returned, and shredded books. There were false starts to a couple of stories and novels, a few rejections along the way, and some critical letters from readers. A child wrote, "I just read your book. The first page was the best part." Then there was that protracted work stoppage, as if my characters had organized and gone out on strike.

Once, in my fifties, I gave a reading at a small college in New Jersey. Afterward, a frail-looking elderly woman approached me and introduced herself. She was Miss Fredericks, my former third-grade teacher! I'm afraid I startled her with an embrace, and then blurted out my thanks for that crucial early support, for telling my mother that I showed promise. She merely looked amused. "Oh, honey," she said, patting my arm. "I told that to all the mothers."

In therapy, we investigated the disappointments and the losses as a possible source of my writing block. Those first champions, my parents, were gone, as was the power of Miss Frederick's prophecy, and it was getting harder and harder to feel inspired. On top of everything else, that most significant age—the digital age—loomed, a threat to actual (as opposed to virtual) bound and beautiful books. Perhaps it was a good time to bow out. So why did I feel so resistant to quitting, so bereft at the very idea? People retire from other jobs with a modicum of grace and a gold watch. Unlike Gerald Monroe, I was still ambitious, but it wasn't as if hordes of fans were clamoring for my next novel. And maybe I just didn't have Estelle Parsons's spirit and durability.

My therapeutic goal gradually changed to simple acceptance of the fact that my writing life was over. The therapist conceded the impact of the losses, from parents to optimism to language, and allowed that I might never write the way I had in the past. Perhaps I'd have to accommodate a new style and different content. But she said that everything I'd told her during our sessions had taken the shape of a *narrative*, that I was still making stories, in spite of myself. She urged me to put something, anything, down every day and see where it took me. It didn't happen overnight, but as soon as I started writing again—with characters of all ages crowding my head, telling me their stories of love and loss, illness and adultery—I knew that I never wanted to stop. Here are ten thoughts I try to keep in mind with that aim.

1. All art is against death.
2. Writing isn't lonely; not writing is.
3. With each new book, I'm breaking through the ice of another writer's block.
4. I must always try to write something I'd like to read.
5. Everyone's inner life is interesting.
6. I'm lucky to keep living multiple lives: my own and the ones I invent.
7. Jell-O, with its translucent shimmer, gaudy colors, and layered construction, is a better metaphor than a dessert.
8. It's preferable to die with a novel (or a handmade sweater) in progress and the dream of finishing it.
9. Edith Wharton is still being avidly read in her 150th year.
10. Writing, at any age, is a way of discovering what one knows.

ACKNOWLEDGMENTS

Thanks are due the following for permission to reprint in this collection:

"On Craft," transcribed and printed with permission of the author. © O.W. Toad, 2012. Delivered by Margaret Atwood at the 2012 AWP Annual Conference & Bookfair in Chicago, IL.

Excerpts from a memoir-in-progress, *The Cruel Country*, by Judith Ortiz Cofer.

"Working on the Ending," by Gail Godwin from the *New York Times*, December 12, 2010, © 2010 The New York Times. All rights reserved. Used by permission and protected by the Copyright Laws of the United States. The printing, copying, redistribution, or retransmission of this Content without express written permission is prohibited.

"Presbyopia," from *Waiting for My Life* by Linda Pastan, copyright © 1981 by Linda Pastan. "Ethics," copyright © 1981 by Linda Pastan; "Sometimes," copyright © 1995 by Linda Pastan; and "Old Woman," copyright © 1978 by Linda Pastan, all from *Carnival Evening: New and Selected Poems, 1968–1998*, by Linda Pastan. "50 Years" and "Firing the Muse," from *Queen of a Rainy Country* by Linda Pastan; copyright ©

1994 by Special Rider Music. "White Rabbit" by Grace Slick, © 1966, 1994 by Irving Music, Inc. (BMI).

I also want to thank Carole Oles, Sandra Gilbert, and Elinor Wilner, whose support in the "Women Writers of a Certain Age" panels helped lead us to this collection; all those older women writers who could not find the time to contribute but cheered us on; Peter Ruppert, always my first and gentlest reader; and our editors Mary Laur and Carol Fisher Saller at the University of Chicago Press, whose patience, enthusiasm, and indefatigable skills have brought this book to light.

J.B.

CONTRIBUTORS

Born in New York City, *Julia Alvarez* spent the first ten years of her life in her family's native country, the Dominican Republic. In 1960, her family was forced to flee to the United States because of her father's involvement in a plot to overthrow dictator Trujillo. Alvarez has been practicing the craft of writing for over forty years. She has brought a variety of work to readers of all ages, including novels, like *How the García Girls Lost Their Accents* and *In the Time of Butterflies*; picture books; the Tía Lola stories for middle readers; novels for young adults; collections of poetry, including *The Woman I Kept to Myself*; and nonfiction, most recently *A Wedding in Haiti* in 2012. With her husband, Bill Eichner, she founded Alta Gracia, a sustainable farm and literacy center in the Dominican Republic. Currently, she is a writer in residence at Middlebury College in Vermont.

Margaret Atwood is the author of more than fifty books of fiction, poetry, and critical essays. Her newest novel, *MaddAddam*, the follow-up to her 2003 Giller Prize finalist, *Oryx and Crake*, was published in the fall of

2013. Other recent publications include the nonfiction *In Other Worlds: SF and the Human Imagination* (2011); *Wandering Wenda and Widow Wallop's Wunderground Washery* (2011), a children's book; and *Payback: Debt and the Shadow Side of Wealth* (2008). Additional titles include the 2000 Booker Prize–winning *The Blind Assassin*; *Alias Grace*, which won the Giller Prize in Canada and the Premio Mondello in Italy; *The Robber Bride, Cat's Eye, The Handmaid's Tale, The Penelopiad,* and *The Tent*. Margaret Atwood was born in Ottawa and currently lives in Toronto with writer Graeme Gibson.

Madeleine Blais was awarded a Pulitzer Prize in feature writing while working at the *Miami Herald*. She teaches at the University of Massachusetts in Amherst and has been a visiting writer at many other institutions, including Goucher, Warren Wilson, Florida International University, and the American University in Bulgaria. She has contributed to many newspapers, including the *Boston Globe*, the *Washington Post*, the *Chicago Tribune* and the *New York Times Magazine*. Her books include *In These Girls Hope Is a Muscle*, finalist for a National Book Critics Circle Award and voted one of the top one hundred sports books of the twentieth century by ESPN, and *Uphill Walkers*, a family memoir which won a Massachusetts Book Award in nonfiction and the Ken Book Award from the National Alliance on Mental Illness.

Rosellen Brown is the author of ten books, five of them novels, *The Autobiography of My Mother, Tender Mercies* (not the movie!), *Civil Wars, Before and After* (of which there *was* a movie), and *Half a Heart*. Her three books of poetry include *Cora Fry's Pillow Book*, and she has published a miscellany of essays, poetry, and stories, and a book of stories, *Street Games*. Her work has appeared frequently in *Best American Short Stories* and *O. Henry Prize Stories* and *Pushcart Prizes*. She teaches in the MFA in Writing program at the School of the Art Institute of Chicago.

Judith Ortiz Cofer is the author of *The Poet Upstairs*, a picture book; *A Love Story Beginning in Spanish*, poems; *Call Me Maria*, *The Meaning of Consuelo*, and *If I Could Fly*, YA novels; *An Island Like You*, a YA collection of stories; *Woman in Front of the Sun: On Becoming a Writer*, a collection of essays; *The Line of the Sun*, a novel; *Silent Dancing*, a collection of essays and poetry; *The Latin Deli: Prose and Poetry*; and other works of fiction, nonfiction, poetry, and children's books. Her current project is a memoir, *The Cruel Country: A Cultural Elegy*. She is the Regents and Franklin Professor of English and Creative Writing at the University of Georgia.

Toi Derricotte is the author of five books of poetry, the newest of which, *The Undertaker's Daughter*, was published in 2011, and a literary memoir, *The Black Notebooks*, which won the 1998 Anisfield-Wolf Book Award for Nonfiction and was a New York Times Notable Book of the Year. Her honors include the 2012 Paterson Poetry Prize for Sustained Literary Achievement and the 2012 PEN/Voelcker Award for Poetry for a poet whose distinguished and growing body of work represents a notable presence in American literature. With Cornelius Eady, she cofounded Cave Canem Foundation, North America's premier "home for black poetry."

Gail Godwin is a three-time National Book Award finalist and the bestselling author of thirteen critically acclaimed novels, including *A Mother and Two Daughters*, *The Good Husband*, *Father Melancholy's Daughter*, *Evensong*, and *Flora*. She is also the author of *The Making of a Writer: Journals, 1961–1963*, the first of two volumes, edited by Rob Neufeld. She has received a Guggenheim Fellowship, National Endowment for the Arts grants for both fiction and libretto writing, and the Award in Literature from the American Academy of Arts and Letters. She lives in Woodstock, New York.

Patricia Henley is the author of four collections of stories and two novels. Her first novel, *Hummingbird House,* was a finalist for the National Book Award. Engine Books published her fourth collection of stories, *Other Heartbreaks,* in 2011. Her work has appeared in the *Atlantic Monthly, Ploughshares, The Pushcart Prize Anthology, Best American Short Stories, Smithsonian Magazine,* and other anthologies and journals. She lives in Cincinnati.

Erica Jong grew up in Manhattan and majored in writing and literature at Barnard College. She received her MA in eighteenth-century English literature from Columbia University and left before finishing her PhD to write *Fear of Flying,* which has sold more than twenty-seven million copies worldwide. In the four decades since *Fear of Flying,* she's written twenty-three books, including fiction, nonfiction, and poetry. She has become one of the most evocative poets of her generation. Her work is honored all over the world. She is married to attorney Kenneth David Burrows, and they have four daughters: Molly, Samantha, Simone, and Colette.

Marilyn Krysl's poems, Alicia Ostriker writes, are "funny, funky, tragic, brave, lyrical, humane, political and full of surprises . . . and she is still writing the liveliest sestinas in America." Her fiction has appeared in *Best American Short Stories* 2000 and *O. Henry Prize Stories. Dinner with Osama* won the Richard Sullivan Prize and Foreword Magazine's 2008 Book of the Year Bronze Medal. She has worked for Peace Brigade International in Sri Lanka and volunteered at Mother Teresa's Kalighat Home for the Destitute and Dying in Calcutta. *Swear the Burning Vow: Selected and New Poems* (2009) is her tenth collection of poetry.

Maxine Kumin's seventeenth poetry collection, *Where I Live: New and Selected Poems 1990–2010,* won the Los Angeles Times Book Prize in

2011. Her final collection, *And Short the Season,* is scheduled for publication in the spring of 2014. Kumin's awards include the Pulitzer and Ruth Lilly Poetry Prizes, the Poets' Prize, and the Harvard Arts and Robert Frost Medals. A former New Hampshire and United States poet laureate, she and her husband live on a farm in the Mink Hills of Warner, New Hampshire, where they raised horses for forty years and enjoyed the companionship of several rescued dogs.

Honor Moore is author of the memoir *The Bishop's Daughter* (National Book Critics Finalist, LA Times Favorite Book of the Year), *The White Blackbird: A Life of the Painter Margarett Sargent by Her Granddaughter* (New York Times Notable Book), and three collections of poems, *Red Shoes, Darling,* and *Memoir.* For Library of America she edited *Amy Lowell: Selected Poems* and *Poems from the Women's Movement* (Oprah Summer Reading Pick). She lives in New York City, where she teaches on the graduate writing faculty at the New School.

Alicia Ostriker is a poet and critic. Her thirteenth poetry collection, *The Book of Seventy,* received the 2009 National Jewish Book Award for Poetry. Her most recent collection is *The Book of Life: Selected Jewish Poems 1979–2011,* for which she has received the Paterson Award for Sustained Literary Achievement, and she has twice been a finalist for a National Book Award. As a critic, Ostriker is the author of several books on poetry and on the Bible, including *The Nakedness of the Fathers: Biblical Visions and Revisions* (1994), a combination of midrash and autobiography; and *For the Love of God: The Bible as an Open Book* (2009), a set of essays. Ostriker teaches in the low-residency MFA program in Poetry and Poetry in Translation at Drew University.

Linda Pastan grew up in New York City, graduated from Radcliffe College in 1954, and received an MA from Brandeis University. She has published thirteen volumes of poetry, most recently *Traveling Light*. Two of these books have been finalists for the National Book Award, one for the Los Angeles Times Book Prize. Pastan was poet laureate of Maryland from 1991 to 1995. She taught for several years at American University and was on the staff of the Bread Loaf Writer's Conference for twenty years. She has won numerous awards, including the Radcliffe Distinguished Alumni Award and the Maurice English Award. In 2003 she won the Ruth Lilly Poetry Prize for lifetime achievement. Pastan lives with her husband in Potomac, Maryland. They have three children and seven grandchildren.

Edith Pearlman's story collection *Binocular Vision* (2011) won awards from the National Book Critics Circle, the Boston Authors' Club, and the University of Hartford (the Edward Lewis Wallant Award) and was a finalist for the National Book Award in fiction, the Story Prize, and the Los Angeles Times Award in fiction. Pearlman also received the 2011 PEN/Malamud Award for excellence in short fiction, honoring her four collections of stories: *Vaquita, Love among the Greats, How to Fall,* and *Binocular Vision.* She has published more than 250 pieces of short fiction and nonfiction in big-city newspapers, anthologies, and periodicals, including the *Atlantic, Commentary, Yankee,* the *American Scholar, Orion, Smithsonian,* and the *New York Times* travel section. Her work has appeared in *Best American Short Stories,* the *O. Henry Prize Stories,* the *Pushcart Prize Stories, Best Stories from the South,* and *Best Non-Required Reading.*

Hilda Raz is Luschei Professor Emerita at the University of Nebraska–Lincoln and past editor of *Prairie Schooner.* She has published many books, among them *All Odd and Splendid* and *Trans* (Wesleyan Poetry Series) and the nonfiction book *What Becomes You,* with Aaron Raz Link (University of Nebraska Press), a finalist for the Lambda Literary

Award. She is founding director of the PS Book Prizes and remains on the literary board. She is now director of the University of New Mexico poetry series, poetry editor of *Bosque*, a literary journal, and a member of the board of Arbor Farms Press. She lives in Placitas, New Mexico.

Jane Smiley is the author of many works of fiction and nonfiction, including *A Thousand Acres, The Greenlanders, The Man Who Invented the Computer, Moo, Horse Heaven*, and *Ten Days in the Hills*. She lives in California.

Laura Tohe is Diné. She is Sleepy Rock clan born for the Bitter Water clan. A librettist and an award-winning poet, her books include *No Parole Today, Making Friends with Water* (chapbook), *Sister Nations* (edited), *Tséyi, Deep in the Rock*, and *Code Talker Stories* (oral history). Her commissioned libretto, *Enemy Slayer: A Navajo Oratorio*, made its world premiere in 2008 and was performed by the Phoenix Symphony Orchestra. Plans are to expand *Enemy Slayer* into an opera. She is Professor with Distinction in Indigenous Literature at Arizona State University.

Hilma Wolitzer is the author of several novels, including *An Available Man, The Doctor's Daughter, Summer Reading*, and *Hearts*; four books for children; and a fiction-writing guide, *The Company of Writers*. Among her honors are grants and awards from the Guggenheim Foundation, the National Endowment for the Arts, the American Academy of Arts and Letters, and the Poets & Writers/Barnes & Noble Writers for Writers Award. She has taught in the writing programs at Columbia University and NYU, at the Writers Workshop at the University of Iowa, and at the Bread Loaf Writers Conference. She lives in New York City.